Sun-Drenched Days, Two-Blanket Nights is a collection of thirty-five essays and sketches, most of which were first published 1983-93.

Arranged chronologically, the stories draw on a variety of outdoor experiences for their subject matter. Come along and meet Emma, the farmer's wife who teaches valuable lessons to a young pheasant hunter; Holly, a friend's beloved Labrador retriever; the Fishscales, ruthless innkeepers who prey on hapless tourists; the Hill which challenges a rusty skier; Moses; the Grousemobile; and an $1800 woodcock.

At times humorous, at times thoughtful, at times thought-provoking, these essays prove once and for all that outdoor writing can indeed become outdoor *literature*.

D1157888

Also by Tom Carney:

Natural Wonders of Michigan

Sun-Drenched Days, Two-Blanket Nights

A Sportsman Takes Note

by Tom Carney

Illustrations by Fred Abels

Partridge Pointe Press

Portions of this book first appeared, in slightly different form, in the *Oakland Press* and the *Advisor Newspapers*.

Cover design: Gail Dennis
Cover art: Fred Abels

ISBN 0-9637085-6-2

Printed in the United States of America.

10   9   8   7   6   5   4   3

*This book is dedicated
to the memory of
Richard E. Carney.*

*Illustrations are dedicated to
Jerry Pleysier
and to the memory of
Jamie Bates.*

Acknowledgements

"A great man is coming to my house to eat," writes Emerson. "I do not wish to please him. Rather, I wish that he should want to please me."

That quote always confused me, until I met some people who are truly great. Then I understood. Instead of expecting special treatment, a great person will make others feel as if they are the special ones.

In the thirteen years that I've been free-lancing, I've been fortunate to meet four people who meet this criterion, four who, while at the top of their respective fields, nevertheless made this commoner feel important: humorist Patrick F. McManus, baseball broadcaster Ernie Harwell, writer Tom Huggler, and wildlife artist Jim Foote.

McManus willingly teaches, shares. Harwell exhibits true concern for helping others. Huggler, the nicest guy you'd ever want to meet, is polite, giving, and is blessed with no small degree of forbearance. And it's impossible to mention Jim Foote without mentioning his wife Joanne. Together they are his art business; they come as a pair. And as a pair, they've been making lots of people feel very special for a long time. It's impossible to think of the Footes without having other words come to mind, terms like graciousness, hospitality, good will, and friendship.

Another source of inspiration is colleague Joan Sanders whose high standards for both literature and humor provide a constant challenge.

And it's a sure bet that this book would not have been completed if not for the technical assistance from Gary Barfknecht, and the encouragement, counseling, insights, input, and plain old elbow grease from designer Gail Dennis.

Finally, Maureen Carney. From the moment we met she's been my partner, my editor, my muse. And—though it took me years to realize it—from the moment we met if I ever wanted to behold a great person in the fullest sense of Emerson's meaning, I only had to look her way.

Introduction

If you spend any amount of time at all in the outdoors, it won't take long before you start to take note.

You'll notice the late twentieth century reality which teaches that the quality of the trip can no longer be measured in direct proportion to the weight of the game bag or fish stringer. You'll realize, too, that playing as great a role in your good times as do an appreciation of nature and development of passable skills, are a similar development of your sense of humor and an infatuation with fine gear and time-polished companions. If you are a singular breed of outdoors person, you'll list purebred hunting dogs under "companions."

You'll notice, too, that the literature you prefer both reflects and reinforces these understandings you've cultivated.

Now, I don't pretend to be an expert or to have lived a life vastly more interesting than you have. I don't live tucked away in the wilderness, and I haven't traveled world-wide in search of adventures in outdoor recreation. If anything, I am probably vastly similar to you: a child of the suburbs, I have to wring as much enjoyment and fulfillment from my infrequent trips afield as I can.

For the last several years, however, I've been compelled to savor such experiences as they occur, for good fortune led me to part-time positions as a columnist with two newspapers in southeast Michigan. While the columns have appeared in the "Sports" sections, and while their topics are, ostensibly, "the outdoors," additional good fortune has hooked me up with editors who have allowed my creativity to roam and to sneak onto side trails more often than not.

The result has been over four hundred columns. From those

four hundred, I've culled little more than thirty which, coupled with some other essays, I hope are worthy of a wider audience. And those are the pieces included in this book.

If we are alike in other ways, then perhaps we share a mutual appreciation for the type of writing that is concise but meaningful, seriously written but not necessarily serious. And if we look for similar designs in the recreation literature we prefer, then the following vignettes, these brief sketches from a variety of outdoors experiences, will provide you entertainment, perhaps some insights, and, I hope, some smiles.

Tom Carney
July 1993

Contents

The Bond *13*

Emma *17*

He Liked to Call Me "Bub" *20*

Ray *23*

Saving Face *26*

Aging Avoidance 101 . . . . *29*

The Morel of the Story *32*

Stream of Conscious *35*

Life and Death in a Metal Band *38*

Farewell to the Grousemobile *41*

Incident at Fishscale's *45*

End of the Line *48*

The Hill *51*

The $1800 Woodcock *54*

Spit Take *57*

Old Friend *60*

A Treasure's Time Has Come *62*

Paddy *65*

The Modified Grand Slam *68*

Passing the Torch *70*

Final Cast *73*

Illuminations *77*

The Comforts of Home *80*

Autumn on the Wing *83*

Face-off at the Blue Wedgie *88*

Holly *91*

Good Times, on Ice *94*

Equilibrium in Spring *98*

Maggie *101*

Reins of Terror *104*

The Road Taken *107*

Summer School *111*

Early Autumn Lullaby *114*

At Home, Alone *117*

Hymns and Libations *120*

The Bond

I 'd like to say a few words about my puppy, Paddy.

I like Paddy just fine, but Yeats was. . . . I know Paddy is a puppy, but Yeats never. . . . Yeats didn't. . . .

I have difficulty, it seems, lately, speaking about Paddy without mentioning Yeats.

Yeats, named for the Irish poet, was a beautiful Irish setter. I got him from the local humane society the day after Easter, 1977. Though he was definitely a purebred setter, there was no way I could trace his roots, for the society destroys all papers to prevent people from breeding the dogs. I didn't know his birthdate, but I always celebrated it on Easter, for it was at that time of the year that I had given him a new life. When I got him, he was four years old.

He was a cast-off I had rescued from certain death. For four years, he'd had a life of his own, developing his own style. I knew as little about him as he did of me.

But, by God, we had a bond.

Paddy is a classically marked English field setter. He was given to me by a friend. Paddy's parentage is absolutely blue-chip for one who wants a dog teeming with finely tuned grouse hunting genes. Paddy was born on my own birthday, March 9. What's more, I brought him home on the 49th day, the day "they" all say is the optimum for forging the bond.

"Forge" is a great word for it, too, for I have sweat like a blacksmith, both physically and emotionally, trying to establish that deeper level of understanding between us, the bond.

The bond. That mystical, psychic link that's often used as a yardstick to gauge the best of men and the best of dogs. More important than being able to boast about your dog's excellent work afield is the opportunity to praise the bond you two have formed; indeed, some scribes will have you believe that without "the bond," there can be no good field work.

I feel tremendous pressure to be able to brag of this bond between Paddy and me. Perhaps I fear having to admit that neither of us is the best of our breed. Worse yet, I fear having to admit failure if he is the best, and I am not.

I felt no such anxiety with Yeats. But I didn't need to. He was a $20 dog and I, a neophyte who realized Yeats would be more pet than hunter.

Nevertheless, Yeats and I understood one another. I think I read his moods. I know he read mine. He wasn't a typical Irish if that means "hard-headed"; he was if it means "fun loving" and "totally dedicated to his master." And I was just as dedicated.

Yeats hunted, not well if you consult only the scorecard, but that doesn't matter. He loved it. Pure and simple. He was the embodiment of enthusiasm and a pure joy to watch. Even casting prejudices aside, I can honestly say that I have never seen a more handsome, regal looking dog than Yeats. He was, quite literally, brilliant, as he'd lope effortlessly through a field, his coat shining golden with the sun.

That's the only specific I want to recollect. The rest are locked in my heart. The more I share, the fewer I'll have left to cling to myself. And the memories I grasp are all that are left of Yeats.

Yeats died last September, a week before opening day, upon returning home from a one-half mile jog he'd begged me to take him on.

For four months I closed myself off. At home, I kept silent. At work, I closed my door at every opportunity. I think I hunted just to be alone.

But it wasn't really hunting; it was like some bad medicine I had to take. My shoulders ached with the burden of Yeats's memory I carried afield with me. Hunting was an empty, hollow chore, not the unbridled pleasure he'd helped create.

I spent those four months breaking the bond with Yeats, or so I thought.

In January, my friend told me his English setter had been bred and would probably whelp in March. He knew I wanted a top-notch grouse dog. A puppy, if I wanted, would be ready to come home with me at the end of April. I spent the next four months, and the subsequent four, forging the bond with Paddy, or so I thought.

My first clue should have come from the name I chose. I could have called him "Pat" for "pa'tridge"; "Patrick" ("the noble born"); or "Patroclus," the dearest friend of the Greek hero Achilles; all those meanings rolled into one. Instead, I chose the IRISH derivative of the name.

But Paddy hasn't proven himself to be a dear friend, or noble, or even mildly interested in the game bird in whose nickname he was baptized, and he's nearly six months old!

Paddy isn't the gentleman Yeats was with guests. Paddy refuses to be totally housebroken while Yeats came already trained. Paddy insists on chewing things and engaging in socially unacceptable behavior. Yeats behaved himself.

Paddy always wants to play, but Yeats would leave me alone when I didn't want him to bother me. Paddy constantly begs for dinner scraps, even though he's never been fed from the table. At dinner time, Yeats used to go lie down in the living room. Paddy, his excellent heritage notwithstanding, has turned out to be as hard-headed as his Irish cousin is supposed to be, but, you will recall, Yeats wasn't, of course.

Paddy's heard the command "NO!" since the first day he's been with me, but each time I yell it to him, he reacts as if he's hearing it for the first time, a word from a foreign language. If he obeys any command at all, he does so at his leisure, because it suits him and not in order to please me.

I tell him "SIT," and he runs to me. I set up a broom handle across two boxes and tell him "JUMP," and he sits. I tell him "STAY," and he follows. I tell him "COME ALONG," and he stays.

I'm working as hard as I can. But what about him? Isn't this bonding business supposed to be a two-way street? Isn't he supposed to be making some of the effort, too? I swear, the only thing he tries to do is to thwart my every effort.

Okay, to be fair, I should admit that when I come home, Paddy is really excited to see me. And he won't let me go to any room of the house without his being there, too. And he doesn't like to stay outside for long if I'm not there. And he does come to my whistle when we go afield. And he has been doing a good job fetching things in the yard. Whoops, I almost forgot: he has smoothly become accustomed to the sound of a shotgun. And he is curled at my feet as I write this. But, I don't know. He's just not like Yeats at all.

That's the key, I've been told. He's *not* Yeats. Let him be Paddy. Let him be Paddy the Puppy for now. Let him grow into his doghood. Let him grow into his role as your bond-mate.

Well, all I can say is he better start growing pretty soon and at a rapid pace. I'm getting tired of providing all of the cohesion in this bond.

Why, just the other day, he and I were driving back from a "training session" at a local state game area. This "session" had involved my listening to him run all around me and my calling him in to tell him how excited he'd be if he would have been in front of me where he belongs and could have seen the woodcock I kicked up.

We came to a stoplight in a small town.

In the car, I kept telling him to lie down, which he, characteristically, interpreted as "Roam around the car, Paddy, and jam my elbow so I can hardly drive in a straight line." I gave him a slight curse and shoved him from the seat to the floor. Checking my frustration as best I could, I swallowed and just looked around.

In a parking lot on the corner, an Irish setter, not unlike Yeats in size, was playfully jumping near his master. Immediately, I felt a pang, and pain surged through my spirit as it always does now when I see an Irish setter.

My thoughts overtook my feelings for a few moments. It was then that I understood: it's not only the forging of a bond that must be completed, and it isn't only Paddy who needs to grow.

Emma

OCTOBER 1984

The snow clung to my shotgun and soaked my jacket, gloves, and even the inside of the Grousemobile, a subtle reminder that not all pheasant hunts are spent romping through fields made golden by a beaming sun. And so, I was chased home earlier than planned.

On the road, I'm easily lulled and, before long, I faced a parade of memories much like the leaves that were supposed to dance down the Main Streets of these Thumb o' Michigan towns at this time of year. And I find it impossible to cogitate about pheasant hunting without begetting images of Emma, Joseph's wife: hefty, open-armed, gentle.

Once home, I am cared for by Maureen, who has developed a menu to complement my reveries. The steaming chili serves as one more reminder of Emma, and I surrender to the montage which endures as the memory of a perfect day's hunt.

Emma and Joseph are friends of my mother's parents. On the first Saturday of pheasant season, my father, his friend Corky, and I visit their farm, only five miles north of Detroit's city limits.

The first to welcome us is Emma. She is a big woman, about 5'8" and stocky. Her graying yet still dark hair is pulled back tightly into a plain bun, leaving only her wire-rimmed eyeglasses to break up the severity of her stern German face.

That presentation seems more of a mask than anything, for when she smiles, which she does often, that forbidding image dissolves into cordial components: flashing teeth, full-rounded happy cheeks, and crow-footed slits behind the lenses.

She wears a long-sleeved, dark dress with a white apron covering. Her sturdy calves are emphasized by thick, dark nylons which by noon will be rolled to her ankles as she straddles the birds she'll be plucking for Joseph and us.

These days Emma seems to exist only for us. She calls us "my boys," and my father and Corky call her "Ma." I don't, because she isn't my mother, until I learn that "Ma" is just short for "Emma." Yet I realize she couldn't have treated her real son Al any better had he survived Korea, were he joining us.

She herds us into her kitchen, the warmth and aroma of which beckon "welcome." While Joseph attends to one last task, Emma offers homemade strudel or coffee cake. It is now that my father presents her with our gift.

Being farmers, she and Joseph are basically self-sufficient. A gift of bread or relish would be a shallow offering on our part. For all of her rugged countenance, however, she does have a passion: hand-painted cups with matching saucers. On Friday, after buying his license at Wolf's Hardware, my father stopped at Berk's five-and-dime to select a present for Emma. She admires it and thanks us several times before we leave for the morning's forage through the fields.

While we are gone, Emma somehow is able to tally who shot and how many times. For our midday rest, she sets out sandwiches and cold drinks on a table in the yard. As we lounge on the cool grass, she asks about and patiently listens to all the details of each shot.

Emma insists that we leave any birds for her to clean before we set out for the afternoon's tour through the corn and the drainage ditches.

For some reason, I've recorded all the hunts at Emma's as "successful," though they all certainly did not produce birds in hand. I think the payoff came each evening.

No matter how lean or meaty are the game bags, no matter how tired your legs, you know things are right as the aroma of her chili transports you those last few yards from the field at dusk.

As you eat her delicious chili, thick and spicy but not enough to make you cry, she cleans and wraps any remaining roosters. Despite any objections, she insists and is genuinely hurt if she can't complete her self-assigned tasks as hostess. One year, my father has to rush home to attend a dinner dance with my mother. Dismayed because we don't even have time to gulp a small bowl, Emma ladles some chili into a Mason jar for us to take. It warms my thighs and hands as I secure it for the ride home.

In those long gone days, Emma was always there. When I was six, she listened as enthusiastically as I spoke when I described the first cock bird I'd ever stumbled upon, the day I brush-busted for my father with a hockey stick/shotgun in hand. She quietly congratulated me, then left me to feel my loss when at seventeen I had bagged my first bird while hunting alone, the autumn after my father had died. Though she is gone and her farm has been transmuted into a Catholic church, a senior citizen residence, and a burgeoning subdivision, it and she remain, warming the spirit from a sealed jar in the lap of memory.

Southern Michigan pheasant hunting the way it is supposed to be: hitting the bedding areas at first light; swinging through a fast rising rooster; waiting at the end of the corn row for a full "thirty Mississippi" count; kicking through the overgrown ditches; rattling the fences; friendship; hospitality; sharing; caring; a kettle of chili.

Some things were taught by my father.

And some were taught by Emma.

He Liked to Call Me "Bub"

OCTOBER 1985

Loss, that sneak of a pickpocket, had struck again with a classic bump and run. He had diverted my attention by chilling with his breath; his icy cold fingers, a chilling drizzle, had soaked my clothes and seized my day afield. Thus stripped, I returned to the car, put Brit in her cage, and recorded as history that opening day's hunt.

A truck stop named "Ruth's" beckoned to my plundered spirit; a warm breakfast sounded right.

I was midway through my coffee with one eye on my car and Brit when the man dashed by the window and in from the rain. With hands in his pants pockets he flapped his arms, like a drumming grouse, to warm up. From his pocket he produced a quarter, a dime, and a nickel, and slapped them on the counter as the waitress greeted him with his coffee. He hunkered down on the stool beside mine and stared into his cup for a few minutes before he spoke.

"Little too wet for bird huntin' today, eh, Bub?"

I agreed that we could have done without the bone-chilling rains and told the man it was even worse in the woods where you also got slapped by the foliage, cold and wet.

We each got a coffee refill, my omelette arrived, and as I ate, he talked about some of his hunting experiences, "back when I was sixty," though he really didn't look any older than his early fifties.

He wore a Detroit Tigers baseball cap which, when readjusted, revealed a salt and pepper brush cut. Rivers of wrinkles flowed from their source—two deep, blue pools framed by wire-rimmed glasses. Beneath his blue nylon warm-up jacket, a plain gray sweatshirt hung on his lanky torso, topping off a pair of loose fitting blue jeans. His running shoes didn't match.

"Durn kids of mine," (he would later tell me with Burton Spiller-like lack of profanity). "They'd toss away money itself if I didn't check up on 'em once'n awhile. Why junk a whole pair of sneakers when only one shoe goes bad? They think I'm crazy, but who's the one who ends up with a free pair of shoes, goin' on three years now? Would ya' call that crazy, Bub?"

"Bub," he liked to call me.

Before long, Brit had settled in her cage, and our short chat had expanded to a four-cup squat-n-gobble. I remember feeling I had nabbed that thief and had recovered my goods. This man had made my day!

We spoke of grouse, the rain, and gun dogs, Thumb country pheasants, and Saginaw Bay duck hunting from sneak boats. He told me he carved his own working decoys; I said I'd tried my hand, unsuccessfully, at decoratives, and just like that, he invited me to his home to see his workshop.

A weather-beaten old canvasback decoy graced the street-level mailbox. Next to that, atop a twenty-foot red pole, perched another box; "Air Mail" he'd painted on its side.

He took me round back and showed off the sneak boat he and his brother had designed and built, all trailered and ready to roll. As he opened the back door of the garage, I commented on the acres and acres of standing corn behind his place.

"Wow! You farm all this by yourself?"

"No. No time," he said. "What with carvin' and huntin' and drinkin' coffee at Ruth's. I've been busier now than before I retired. Ya' know what I mean, Bub? Plus, I never get back from Florida in time to get the fields ready in spring. So, I just lease them out to a local."

We stepped inside the garage that was no longer a garage. His car had been ousted from its parking spot by homemade tables and shelves, a vise bench, raw lumber, several hundred cedar decoy bodies and heads, finished blocks, drawers of eyes, dozens of jars and cans of paints and tints, handmade draw knives and other tools, posters, stuffed models, and five ancient reference texts.

Number six was the man himself, once he started talking. He

reviewed how to build and paint, conducting a mini-seminar in a half-hour's time. By then, however, I felt kind of guilty hanging around: his wife had tried to nudge him along gently a few times; the fourth time, wrath had started a slow, but obvious journey from her lungs to her voice box. So I shuffled around to leaving and said maybe I'd come back and take him grouse chasing sometime.

"Fine with me," he said. "Just stop by and see if I'm here. Ya' might want t'check Ruth's first."

That was the beginning of it. On Saturdays during the season, if I felt like it and didn't have anyone else to hunt with, I'd stop by and ask him to join Brit and me. If he wanted to, he would. Within a few weeks that first year, I had wrangled an invite to go duck hunting on the first Saturday of deer season when other bird seasons closed.

That's how it went for four years. I stopped by when I felt like it, but always that one Saturday in November. He went along with me if and when it suited his purpose. Nothing else. No exchange of phone numbers. No saccharine Christmas cards. No empty promises of sportsmen's club dinners we'd attend so's the wives could meet. It was, in the purest sense of the word, a symbiotic relationship; not at all gilded, nonetheless priceless. Good God! How I enjoyed that man!

Then, the first Saturday of the first fall of the setter, I headed out to the Thumb; the dog full of promise, I, hope. As if on cue, the fingers of chilling rain penetrated my clothes and seized my day. I cursed that crook and resolved to thwart him as I had done years earlier.

Ruth's cheese omelette sounded like a good deal. Besides, this would be a chance to show off the pup.

He wasn't at Ruth's, never appeared, and after three cups I decided to go to his place. What a sight. The "Air Mail" pole had been dropped. The door of the other mailbox had been broken off, along with the head of that old canvasback atop it. The house was vacant; windows, naked; the garage, locked. Behind the garage, the duck boat lay broken, wounded, and twisted halfway off the tire-flattened trailer. The field was unworked, untended.

That was the end of it.

There had been no phone call. No letter. No farewell dinner.

A purr of contentment came with the chilling breath. The icy cold fingers rushed in for a second touch that day.

This time they squeezed.

Ray

A grouse hunter need not explain why he considers the fall of the year as the new beginning. He doesn't spend his New Year's Eve by counting down the Times Square apple, but by checking and packing the gear while his gun dog stays close by, fretting, lest the festivities begin without him.

The two of them might sleep fitfully, each reliving some of those classic moments: the mixed double that one time in their favorite aspen slashing, pinned, flushed, and released, with a couple of warning shots; the pup's burrowing beneath the deadfall to clutch a mouthful of wounded grouse that had run but couldn't hide. The hunter might start in his sleep only moments before the dog yips from his own dreams. For both, the world is coming alive again, and for me that new year, new hope is signalled by Ray.

I wouldn't know Ray if I didn't know Jim; I only see Ray if I see Jim; I usually only see Jim one weekend each fall. Yet in the few years I've been blessed with his acquaintance, Ray has become for me as integral a part of the consecration of the season as the opening salvo of blackberry brandy in grouse camp and sausage gravy and biscuits from "Pappy's" in town. In fact, I've come to take Ray's appearance as the gods' personal blessing on my hunting season.

As ritualistic as things can be, it's the same each year. Jim and I will be sitting down to a morning cup, his setter snarling mine into line. My innards pace as much as my pup does, anxious for the hunt. The light mist lifts slowly from the pond, and a brace of wood ducks darts by.

In the near distance a movement catches my eye. I see Ray strolling from his cabin, and my inner storm is calmed. He carries his own cup, its steam commingling with the mist. Like a banshee, his own setter streaks among the trees and down the path. She waits outside when Ray steps in.

Always a gentleman, Ray first greets me and tells me how fine my dog looks. Then he and Jim fall into their standard discussion: who's gonna' hunt where, how long a particular covert has been left undisturbed, how well the hunt went yesterday afternoon, and the quality of the dogwork of late. In fact, I've never heard the two of them broach any topic other than bird hunting with fine dogs.

As Ray sits there, I am reminded, to a degree, of my father. Ray's hair, white and wavy, is just like my dad's—or like my dad's would have been had he ever let it grow beyond brush-cut length. Ray's eyes, too. Imagine drooping, sad eyes, like a basset hound's, deep, intelligent, kind. Now, color those eyes in a grayish-blue and you can picture the eyes of my father and Ray.

And like a good father, Ray is someone who clearly instructs by example, never telling you what you should do but always showing. You try to establish yourself as part of his world by telling him what you know, prattling on, oblivious to your own nonsense until later experiences prove you wrong.

Ray's so smart he doesn't say a thing, neither correcting your errors nor offering an implied "told you so." You know that he knows, and you wonder to what degree he's labeled you a fool. And you've learned that truly smart people don't have to say anything to prove to others that they're smart. And you can only speculate as to how long it will be until you can apply that criterion to yourself.

Ray's a real gentleman; I know I've said that already, but it bears repeating. He's one of the few people in your life you wish you could be.

He's a sportsman who's studied his quarry well. He is a fine hunter who sets a brisk pace for young 'uns half his age. His keen eye complements those strong legs which in a half-season's time wear out a pair of the best "Brush-tuff" bird pants you can find in the mail order catalogues.

Ray shoots well, giving an "Aw shucks" kind of remark to your praise, but praising you on your lucky hits, sometimes even before the smoke has cleared and you've opened your eyes. He handles gun dogs as well as people, and in this area, too, you can learn an awful lot by keeping your mouth shut.

In a way, Ray is a lot like the ruffed grouse he so ardently pursues. Always, but especially at this time of year, each charges the air with his majesty, dignity, and grace.

Saving Face

OCTOBER 1987

My father-in-law, Charles, is fond of reminding me of his decision that I should have been a lawyer instead of a high school teacher.

"Boy, you're so good at twistin' things around that if you were Custer, the Indians would be honoring you now as their best friend," he's told me on more than one occasion.

What he doesn't understand, however, is that I couldn't have developed that skill unless I first became a teacher. The reason for this is simple: name any other career in which ninety percent of the time you speak to another adult, you are being asked or forced to defend yourself, your actions, or your decisions. After a decade or more of that, anyone would only find it natural.

No problem at work. But I'm finding more and more now that I have to come up with excuses for those times I come up empty-handed on my hunting trips. No, Maureen doesn't hold me up to the light when I return home as Mr. M.T. Gamebag. In fact, the only explaining I ever have to give to her is how come the dog and I always smell the same when we get home, and why he expects to be offered each plate to lick before it goes into the dishwasher.

But the degree of sympathy extended by hunting companions or the amount of bragging employed sometimes strips one of all options. Therefore, I'll offer the following "Excuses for Saving Face."

1. **"My glasses fogged up."**

Some people wear shooting glasses for safety reasons, to keep twigs and branches from scratching their eyes. But I'll tell you what, the specs come in awfully handy when someone is very close to you and kicks up a bird which flies right in front of you and knows you should have dropped it.

2. "I was still dizzy from the blow to my head."

Extremely useful upon missing a shot soon after your father-in-law or other weisenheimer clunks you with his gunstock on the walk from the truck. After all, a hunter must be an opportunist.

3. "I was wiping my glasses."

See explanation to # 1 above.

4. "What bird?"

5. "I didn't shoot because I wasn't sure where you were."

Go ahead. Make 'em feel guilty for gooning you when you only had their safety in mind. (Must be used before all the leaves fall from the trees.)

6. "I was checking my compass."

Same basis as # 1. Also more effective if you make sure you are the only one in the group with a compass; that way, they need you to be checking it. WARNING: Be prepared for using this excuse. Before heading into the thick stuff, be sure to announce to everyone, "Wait a second. Let me get a compass bearing, here."

7. "Its wheeze sounded like yours, so I started talking to it."

When you didn't shoot the 12-point buck your partner says he'd spooked your way.

8. "He gave us the slip."

One of my favorites. Useful in many situations: grouse never flushes, flushes out of range, or flushes before you've finished tripping over a deadfall; a deer "vanishes" while you are tracking him in fresh snow; your dog makes a fine point, but nothing is there. NOTE: Be sure that your companion is absolutely clear of the immediate area and can in no way dispute your claim. If he can, then refer to #'s 1, 3, 6, or any other applicable excuse.

9. "I was going to the bathroom."

Alternate with # 8. See NOTE contained therein.

10. "It was so cold that the adrenalin couldn't pump through me fast enough for me to shoot in time."

NOTE: Not to be used in temperatures above 25 degrees or

with anyone who has any knowledge of physiology, whatsoever.

11. "I thought you'd have a better shot."

Who could berate an unselfish gentleman?

12. "Scope was fogged up."

Same principle as in # 1 for the deer hunter sitting in a blind.

13. "Your dog looked so beautiful on point that I plumb forgot to shoot."

You've complimented the guy's dog, for crying out loud; plus, the "plumb forgot" bit makes you sound so innocent, you're home free on this one. NOTE: Not to be used in a duck blind when your partner's retriever will look beautiful only after you've shot something for him to retrieve.

14. "I was picking up my hat."

15. "I couldn't get the safety off."

16. "I'd loaded a 'Chap-Stick' instead of a shell."

These last three all carry the same onus as does # 6. Make sure your buddies know you have trouble with your hat or safety, or that you are tending to some chapped lips, well before you head too far away from the car. This way, they can't act as if they didn't know.

17. "I was looking at ducks farther away from the ones you saw."

Not only does it excuse you, but this one also adds a dash of guilt to your partner who obviously wasn't scanning the skies as well as you.

18. "I was just enjoyin' callin' in those ducks for you."

Same basic principles as those behind #'s 11 and 13. Make sure you use the folksy "enjoyin'" for effect. Also, it might be a good idea to actually be able to attract birds with the calls you make.

19. "My doctor says my propensity for protracted nictitation produces an inability to achieve the desired geophysical relationship of a contemporaneous time-order juncture between the avian and spherical phenomena."

Enough big words will usually keep your meaning a secret. But if your buddy has needed to come up with some excuses of his own, he'll know that you have just said, "I can't hit anything with my eyes closed."

20. "I had set down my gun to take a picture of you which I'm sure will get published in *Outdoor Life*."

Better make sure you have a camera along for this one. Better make sure the picture gets published. Or better make sure you find a new hunting partner for next year.

Aging Avoidance 101

APRIL 1988

I'm never gonna get old, and I can prove it!

In my lingo, word choice definitely indicates the relative age of any human male I'm referring to. A "kid" is someone much younger than I. A "man" is someone much older. And a "guy" is someone in my same general age group.

I've noted that the closer a guy gets to middle age, the more he realizes that it's only men who are middle-aged, so he doesn't have to worry yet, even if he's closer to forty now than to eighteen.

Another phenomenon specific to us guys is the fact that each of us in his own way has found a way—or a combination of ways—to avoid getting old. Some guys comb their hair forward or sideways or in whatever direction required to prevent the tops of their heads from getting sunburned. Others try to recapture the "Glory Days" by chasing chicks, or staying involved in sports as fans, coaches, or heroes of recreation league basketball. (No one wants to bowl, yet; that's for men.) Some other guys refurbish classic cars from their youth as if to say, "If I keep this '57 Chevy shiny, then I'll never rust myself."

As for me, I've got my sneakers.

Remember one of the best rituals in the spring of the year, in the spring of your life? Goin' to get your new tennis shoes. Although we didn't play tennis in them—come to think of it, we didn't do too much sneaking around in them, either—but what else do you call them? I'm talking about the times when the best recreational shoe available was the good ol' black canvas high-top with white rubber sidewalls, ventilation holes near the instep, and a product I.D. patch on the inner ankle bone part of the shoe. These were the times before anyone "aerobicized," when the best basketball shoes cost under ten dollars, and when if you said you were going to look at some "Reeboks," people might expect you to watch a film about Australian wildlife. I'm talking about Red Ball Jets, and "Keds, Kids, Keds!" and "P.F. Flyers! They help you to run your fastest and jump your highest!"

There were no specialized shoes for us. No matter what your activity, the sneaks were your chosen and the appropriate footwear. They were your baseball spikes, hoop shoes, and army boots.

They were your brakes and stabilizers when you raced your bike through the field. Your carpenter boots when you built stuff and your mountain climbers when you scaled Miller Hill, all fifteen feet of it. And they were your explorer's boots when you investigated the mine shaft and pond behind the hill. Smelling as bad as you did, they were your constant companions except for the couple of days they'd need to dry out after you got a soaker in the pond. You could wear the sneaks to school and look as if you were pondering the mysteries of math while you were really studying them to imagine what adventures they held for the forthcoming summer.

I found my new sneaks recently while poking through the Atlanta Sports Shop, having gotten into some dry clothes after fishing a steelhead stream whose water was surprisingly and shockingly deeper than wader-high. Imagine my delight when I saw on the shelves actual "P.F. Flyer" boxes which, it turns out, the owner had found while cleaning the upstairs. As soon as I laced them up, I was young again. My father-in-law nearly had a spell as I began climbing trees back in camp. I came close to getting a soaker down by the stream, but jumping my highest, I escaped.

Back home, I wear them all the time. My Rockports and Johnston & Murphys are in dry dock. My principal recently told me not to wear the sneakers to school anymore.

"Why not? Don't you think they're professional enough?"

"That has nothing to do with it," he said. "It's just that too many students are complaining that you spend all classtime looking at the shoes, getting dreamy-eyed, and then asking, 'How long till summer vacation?' "

And it doesn't matter that the dog has pulled his rug to the other side of the bedroom in disgust. When I go to bed, the sneakers drop right there, right next to me. No matter the sneaker odor, there they sit, ready to launch me into the next adventure of this extended springtime.

Why won't I ever get old? That's simple. All this guy has to do is to preserve those sneakers and he will remain a kid. And since he's starting to run more and more like a man, the sneakers will never wear out.

The Morel of the Story

T he day beamed brightly. The woods called lustily. Charles and
I tightened up our boots, sprayed ourselves with bug dope, and
gathered our gear for our spring hunt.

Mid-May is prime hunting time and we wanted to insure our
success. I double-checked to see that my knife was sharp. Charles
brought the instructions and the baskets. Thus armed, we headed
into the forest in search of the elusive Michigan morel.

According to the instructions, "Michigan Morels," a pamphlet
produced by the Michigan Travel Bureau and the DNR, "Department of Natural Resources field workers report counting at least as
many vehicles parked along roads during the spring morel season
as during the November deer hunt."

These hunters can be just as greedy as some deer hunters are
reported to be, too. Why, one slob morel hunter ran up and put his
tag on a Morchella angusticeps just as I had spotted it and made
my move. We had a rough and tumble disagreement until I, being
the gentleman that I am, allowed that maybe he had gotten there
first and had a right to the mushroom. So he released me from the
headlock, gathered the morel into his basket, and went merrily on
his way.

Charles didn't quite know what to make of this scene, this being
his first time on the trail of the mushrooms.

That's another point from the pamphlet: "Finding a veteran
mushroom hunter to lead you on your first ventures is a problem
you must solve for yourself."

Charles was lucky, for I was able to give him the benefit of my expertise, but as he was rubbing the Ben-Gay into my neck, he asked for reassurance of my knowledge.

I had first gone 'shrooming back in the spring of 1985, with then high school senior and all-state basketball star, Jeff McCool of Sterling Heights. We had both ditched—uh—"taken the day off" school, to hit the streams near his parents' northern property in time for the trout opener and to be in the woods for some early season morel hunting. As it turned out, we exchanged seminars. Jeff taught me how to stalk the morels and to make a clean, swift kill. I demonstrated how to exit gracefully from a stream of 42-degree neck-deep water while wearing chest-high waders.

Charles felt better, realizing Jeff's love of the outdoors would have punctuated any lessons he had given. But Charles remained insecure about his own capabilities. Having been experienced only in duck hunting, Charles voiced some concerns:

"I mean, how are we going to tell the difference between a drake and a hen morel? I don't want to take the wrong kind and get a fine from a conservation officer."

Well, I shot him a glance that only a veteran can shoot to a tyro to confront him with his own ignorance. How many times had I told Charles that you don't need a license to hunt morels so no C.O.'s would be checking game baskets. (What I didn't tell him, of course, just to make him feel bad when he does find out, is that the scientific terms for male and female mushrooms are "moes" and "morelettes"—not "drakes" and "hens.") But I did offer him the note: "Don't worry. If you get caught with a 'hen,' (har! har!) just say she charged you and you had to defend yourself from getting gored." That didn't sit too well with Charles.

So, just to be safe, we decided to hunt on our property up in Atlanta—a combination of ridge and low lies, choice mushroom country. Now, morels are difficult to see because they blend in so well with the old fall foliage. Plus, the swarming black flies made us want to hustle through the woods faster than we should have in order to quietly, and thus more efficiently, stalk our prey. As a result, by late afternoon, our game baskets remained empty.

"Well, if you don't get 'em, you don't have to clean 'em," I offered, full of philosophy.

Charles merely gave me a sidelong, considered his lifelong aversion to profanity, and continued scanning the ground.

As darkness approached, he finally found one mushroom and gleefully put it in his basket. We didn't bother to check the pamphlet, for I had remembered seeing something in it that resembled the mushroom we had picked. So we quick-stepped back to camp, sliced it, sauteed it in about a half pound of margarine, and sat back to enjoy our feast.

Boy oh boy! Some people would complain if you hung them with a new rope! As we were leaving the emergency room at the Alpena General Hospital, Chuckie-boy began a song that he sang all the way home:

"I should have gone with someone with more experience! You should have double-checked the booklet, and you would have seen that mushroom listed under the poisonous variety! You must be trying to kill your poor old father-in-law! Why, you dirty cur!"

When he got to the portion of the litany about how it's good that his other son-in-law Jackson is a lawyer so he can sue me for attempted murder and to get me kicked out of the family, I had just about had enough. So I casually mentioned to Charles the only thing I could in order to plant the responsibility firmly where it belonged:

"Don't blame me, Chuckie. You're the one who basketed a morelette!"

Stream of Conscious

There are perhaps worse by-products of a suburban upbringing. But by draping us in shopping malls, subdivisions, and the "I can always move to another town" mentality, the suburbs have stripped us of a sympathy that can never be replaced: the contentment, the oneness, the permanence a person feels because a certain tract of geography has been a constant in his life. It's the identity William Butler Yeats found in Ireland, the love Ansel Adams captured in his photographs of the High Sierra and the Yosemite Valley, the roots Laura Ingalls Wilder sprouted on the prairie, the passion for the St. Clair River that flows through the old man.

Every day, even now as autumn approaches, the old man pulls himself awake before dawn and prepares again to visit the river which stretches for some twenty-seven miles between the U.S. and Canada alongside Michigan's Thumb. He dresses quickly, not because he is sprite but because his outfit is always the same: T-shirt, sweatshirt, khaki work pants, and a pair of running shoes he found in the corner of an upstairs closet after his youngest son had moved out.

His fingers, like sun-dried leather two days after a storm, must be flexed and coaxed into working order for one more day. The man is too impatient to wait for coffee to perk, so he drinks instant, warming those resistant fingers on the mug.

At first light, he goes fishing but doesn't care if he catches fish. His chief target is walleye, referred to locally as "pickerel." By ten he usually has moored his craft in the canal in front of the cottage of his friend's widow. This schedule, he says, makes him happy. He gets the shakes, he says, if he drifts too far from home, from the river.

"Back then, we'd skate on her all winter," he'll say of his younger days.

"The best places to skate were near the air holes. You'd get so it would be blowin' a gale out there and 'Swoosh!' the water would rush out of those holes and freeze up real nice. That way we'd always have fresh, smooth, clean ice. You could probably find safer places to skate, but then you'd always have to shovel the snow away.

"You learned real fast to skate on the upstream edge of the holes so that if you went through, you'd have a chance to grab onto the side before you reached the end and were pulled under. . .

"In spring the break-up would come all at once, and 'Swish!' the ice would be gone. Then we'd put away the skates and take out our swim suits. . .

"My mother always thought I was in good hands with my brother Bill and the Smith boys because they were older. She had no idea they were trying to kill me, those dirty curs.

"Since I was the smallest, I was the one who had to test everything before they'd try it, like the ice on the canals, or the ride on the pulley we had strung between the tops of two trees.

"I even tested the diving gear once. Why, sure. They took a five-gallon paint can and rigged a hose to it. The other end of the hose was hooked to a hand pump. Then they put that bucket over my head and tied it to my shoulders. I had to hold onto a couple of bricks to pull me down.

"I could breathe okay until I got about twelve feet out, just to the edge of the drop off. They must have got concerned with something else and forgot to pump. And I just dropped those bricks and popped up to the surface. . .

"The *Tashmoo* was a big boat for back then, about a four hundred foot side wheeler. And when she was pulling out from the dock, they only had so much room to maneuver. They'd have to back her up to get her nose out into the current. Then they'd notch her into forward. But there was that moment when the wheel wasn't turning, kind of like when you're rocking a car between forward and reverse to get it out of the snow. You were a real hero if you could dive in and touch the paddle wheel before she started turning again.

"When she did, though, she'd make a big whirlpool. The trick was to jump into that whirlpool and get dragged down to the bottom. And that was fun. Bill got crossed up once down there and I had to go in after him.

"Why, I shoulda' been killed about a hundred times out there with all the stunts we pulled. Now, I'm scared of my own shadow. But we didn't think anything of it back then. . .

"Mother was pretty good at figurin' out when Dad's ship would be passing, and he'd give a couple of blasts on the big horn when he reached Robert's Landing. Then we'd all run down to the river with our towels and wave to our dad as he passed.

"There were times we'd be fishin' and if we got thirsty, we'd just dip a cup into the river."

The old man can no longer drink from the river of his youth. The waters have changed, though the current has endured. Heavy boat traffic makes weekend fishing unappealing. Hot water discharged from upstream factories keeps the river flowing all year. The best friends of his life are all gone, one, by one, by one. So too, his wife; and on that chilling gray winter day she was laid to rest, the river passed along, chilled and gray, yet impassive, austere, unwavering.

Children they had, more than a dozen. And like the ice floes which break apart and wash away in spring, each child has left at his own pace. The old man himself teases with talk of a move to Florida, northern Lower Michigan, or even the Upper Peninsula, and on the surface it appears he has no reason to stay.

But the current runs deep, as deep as memory.

The morning sun blazes a trail through the mist and soon stands glorious, warming. Gulls and terns swarm and dive, nature's convoy for his little skiff. A few pickerel shake his hand, not enough for a limit, but plenty for a meal. He hails the sailors on a couple of big boats. He greets some fellow fishermen and lies to some others. The steady breeze assures a good drift. The deep blue of the sky is reflected in both the blissful yet snag-ridden river and his now happy but often sad eyes.

It is now that the child of the suburbs understands why he will never leave.

The man defines the river.

The river sustains the man.

Life and Death in a Metal Band

FEBRUARY 1989

T his all started with a certificate sent from the U.S. Fish and
Wildlife Service.

We all can tuck ourselves neatly away in suburbia and not
worry about the sick, the homeless, the abused. To alleviate any
feelings of responsibility or guilt that tug at our hearts, we can
simply and mindlessly check off a donation to the United Fund from
our pay during the Torch Drive. Things are sterile and simple for
us. Neat, sweet, and clean, we can deal with a problem without
thinking about it.

The next level is to decide on the top charities you'll support, sit
down, write each check, address an envelope and a note of explanation, and send the contribution off yourself. That's when involvement begins, when you start to imagine the pain that many people
have to endure.

If the reality of life's cruelty is too much for you to deal with on
a more personal basis, your involvement ends there. If you have a
stronger resolve, you volunteer, trying to help those in need by
giving something much more precious than money: your time.

If you are weak, you ignore the situation entirely, failing to
acknowledge its existence.

That last way is the same type of head-in-the-sand approach to another cruel aspect of life that anti-hunters take. "We think hunting is disgusting," they seem to say, "and so should everyone else. Animals should not have to suffer because some vain people enjoy killing them."

The double fallacy in that argument results from the self-righteous assumptions that hunters actually enjoy killing and that the anti-hunter does nothing to harm the animals.

We hunt, to be sure, because we enjoy it. But the kill is only a minor part of the experience, and you'd be hard-pressed to hear a sportsman say he enjoys the killing. Most will tell you that they love nature and animals. Though that argument might sound contradictory, it is, nevertheless, valid. "Do I contradict myself?" says Walt Whitman. "Very well then I contradict myself (I am large, I contain multitudes.)"

The hunter is not the only one being contradictory. So, too, is the anti. No person living in our world today can exist without causing the destruction of thousands of animals. Your hamburger didn't just float down from heaven. The parking lots, shopping malls, subdivisions, factories, and offices all sit where animals once lived.

But by singling out the hunter as the target of their ire, the animal rightists are not only ignoring the greater enemy of wildlife, the developers. They are also implying that destroying animals is acceptable if some kind of profit can be made from it. And they are rejecting any type of responsibility for providing for wildlife other than in their efforts to keep people from eating game animals that they've legally killed.

Yes, the hunter is an easy target because he can be directly linked to the death of an animal. But what must also be admitted is that for the most part it is the hunter who provides funds to safeguard animals and to protect their habitats. It is the hunter above all others who acknowledges man's role in the cruel but inevitable aspect of life which says, "Things die so that others might live."

In this way, the hunter takes full responsibility for the life he has taken, unlike the suburbanite who picks up his meat at a store without giving it a second thought. In this way, the hunter is much like the volunteer who admits to life as it is, accepts a role, and undertakes the duty of helping others by serving meals in an inner-city soup kitchen on Christmas Day.

The certificate I received magnified all that for me. On closing day of duck season this year, three of us got our limits of available ducks, two mallards apiece. One was banded. So I asked the Fish and Wildlife Service for information about her. She was a hen about two and a half years old and had been banded near Linwood, not far from Pinconning, on August 26, 1986, by "Ms. M. Stratz," a DNR employee. Ms. Stratz was sent another certificate informing her of the death of that duck.

Hunters usually reject one anti-hunting ploy, the "Bambi syndrome," so-called because the proponents project an image of game animals as if they exist in a perpetual spring and have human personalities, like in a Disney cartoon. I can usually refute that tack myself. But for goodness sake, I had just received the birth certificate for something I had killed. I can't ignore the tug on the old heart strings.

But that won't stop me from killing again. What it does is to remind that life, all life, is ultimately comprised of tragedy. And as Aristotle tells us, good tragedy should cite pity and fear in the beholder. We pity the animals because they shouldn't have to die. We fear because we know that we, like them, will die. And we realize that in this tragedy, we each must play a role. Because that's life.

In a perfect world, we could practice "shoot and release" hunting. In a perfect world, we would still hunt with fine dogs, fine guns, and fine companions, only the animals wouldn't die when shot. But in a perfect world, we wouldn't have the sick, the homeless, and the abused, either.

Farewell to the Grousemobile

MARCH 1989

The Grousemobile is gone, and I don't feel so hot.

You know how it is when you break up with a girl. You both realize the relationship has run its course. You each find another friend. You're reluctant to extend yourself entirely to the new object of your affection because you still miss the one who is gone, wishing you could be together but knowing all along that the breakup was inevitable. That's how it's been with the Grousemobile.

You see, the Grousemobile was a 1984 Ford Bronco II. It was the only car I ever ordered brand new for myself. We broke up little more than a year ago because I had bought a new mini pickup truck. I'm still not sure why I did it. Sure, the pickup is sleek, black, and comfortable, but I just can't get the Grousemobile out of my mind, or my heart. It's really easy to find faults with the new truck, and I've taken it back no fewer than a dozen times just to get one squeak fixed. Simply put, the truck just is not the G-mobile. People drool over the new vehicle on my arm and ask how I like it. I just mutter something to get away from them.

That Bronco received better care than any other vehicle I'll ever own. I must've changed the oil on her about thirty times. Her odometer's 94,000 miles made things all the more tough when it came time to sell her. Because not only were people leery of buying something so well-used, but also those miles were all mine, recorded mostly in clusters on our many trips during the five and a half years we were together. No one else assumed the helm of the Grousemobile except for those who'd earned the highest degree of trust: my father-in-law Charles, Jackson my brother-in-law, and hunting partner Glenn. Heck, even my wife Maureen only drove it for a total of two hundred miles. And those were on a three thousand mile trip we took one week a few years ago. She knew the high quality of driving skills expected, and she felt sadly lacking. I agreed with her assessment and—red-eyed all the way—took my place in the driver's seat that fitted my form so well.

No one even smoked in her, except the one time in Ely, Minnesota. In celebration and thanksgiving after returning to dry land from the Boundary Waters, I forgot myself and momentarily lit up a stogie before Charles noted and remarked upon my indiscretion.

No one will ever take care of that Bronco as I did.

Among my hunting companions and me, "Let's take the Grousemobile," became as familiar a phrase as have "I thought you checked the compass" and "Desperate times call for desperate measures." And instead of the possessive "my," it was always spoken of as a third person, "the" Grousemobile. And now, it's gone.

So can you blame me if I'm moping?

"I can't believe how emotional you get with your car," Maureen said during my initial period of mourning.

Perhaps with just a touch of envy she added, "You're more upset over selling that Grousemobile than you would be if I left you."

It hurts too much to manufacture a rejoinder. But why bother? She must have an idea of how many times I had set out to buy her flowers, but instead of turning left into the florist, I turned right into the tire center for another rotation and balance.

"And look at this," she continued, noting a thick envelope tucked neatly away on my bookshelf. "You saved the old repair bills like some love letters from an old girlfriend."

"So what?" I snorted as I retrieved them. And geez, did it hurt when I untied the pink ribbon that bound them. My hands shook as I sniffed them once more for the wonderfully blended scent of ink, carbon paper, and grease. My heart trembled as I prepared to read.

Look! Here's the bill for the distributor cap, wires, and new belts and hoses. How I remember that trip. Ol' Charles and I were camped seven miles back from M-28, the "Seney stretch," the highway that runs in a straight line across the heart of Michigan's Upper Peninsula for about forty miles. Except for the railroad tracks, the town of Seney is the only human punctuation along this stretch. Hence, the name. The truck wouldn't start, and we would have faced a long, long hike to the nearest phone if not for the graces of a few good-hearted bear hunters who pulled us out and refused any payment but our thanks.

How about this BIG bill for the new manifold exhaust pipe, power steering unit, and rebuilt front end? How coincidental that they'd all go bad on that one big trip that I had to make up north to get in a couple of interviews. I think she was just playing coy with me, testing the limits of my tolerance. Dames, sheesh!

Oh, here's the receipt for the new tires, supposedly good for 40,000 miles but still functional at 57,000 when I sold the G-mobile. See, Maureen? And flowers would have lasted about a week before dying. Only one day after I purchased them, those tires did a wonderful job keeping us on the road as we headed north for our annual cross-country ski weekend. The snow was extra slick and extra heavy, but the tires—and the truck—never wavered from their duty.

Here's the sweet-scented reminder that the air conditioner bracket, a special ordered part, had arrived. Good. Just two days after Charles and I had left for our trip to Minnesota, a 2600-mile journey without a/c during the hottest summer on record.

What's this? Oh yeah, the note from "le mechanique du Trois Rivieres," for fixing the windshield wipers as we headed for Quebec City aboard "la voiture de la grosse gelinotte." (French Canadian for "Grousemobile," can you tell?) That's right. The wiper motor burned out on the same trip that we had to recharge the battery in Freeport, Maine, after we'd spent the night in the truck at the shrine, L.L. Bean.

Well, this bill isn't as old as the rest. It's from only a couple of months before I dumped her. That carburetor adjustment in Escanaba had cost me more than all the rest of that trip to the U.P. for woodcock. I would've been better off in the long run if I had simply had it rebuilt.

What's this doing in with the bills? It's the receipt for the Harsen's Island ferry. Boy, doesn't that remind me of those great duck hunting trips that last fall? If the cryptic message arrived from Charles, the Grousemobile would spirit me away from work and deposit me onto the Island in less than an hour. On the way out of the building, I'd remove my tie. While on the expressway, I'd put her in "CRUISE" and wrestle out of work shoes and socks into my huntin' socks and slip-on boots. By the time I set down on the island, I'd have changed everything except my pants. And I always made sure that no matter my state of undress or re-dress, I'd always be wearing my camo hat when I first boarded the ferry.

Ah, me. . . .

The guy who bought the Grousemobile was supposed to come over to retrieve a few odds and ends I'd forgotten to take to him. I was hoping to be able to drive her again, once more for old time's sake, maybe even go to get Maureen some flowers. He never showed up.

But I know where he works.

Incident at Fishscale's

F ishscale's Resort on Drummond Isle is the kind of place I'd love to recommend to you, if you're the person responsible for raising my taxes, the one who dented my truck in the K Mart parking lot, or the television program director responsible for the *Webster* reruns.

My pal, John Northrup, and I had been planning our visit for the last three years, trying to time the woodcock flights and the fall perch run so we could make a run of our own and return with full coolers and game bags. The solunar tables, our horoscopes, John's arthritic knee, the wart on the bottom of my right foot, and our wives' permission all congealed in the seventh house of Jupiter, and the apex pointed to 1989 as the year of our trip.

We caught the 9:40 ferry from DeTour Village as it left promptly at 10:36 p.m. After a short crossing and a drive through the absolute darkness, we arrived at the resort by 11:00.

Although Mr. and Mrs. Fishscale were firmly ensconced in their warm beds for the night, they had thoughtfully left a floodlight lit and pointed toward our second-story kitchenette. If not for the light, we might have spent the rest of the night wandering aimlessly, trying to find our room, much like the couple from Ohio whom we beat into the parking lot.

We zipped up the stairway above the bait shop to what we thought was our room. The door was unlocked, and we rushed in. We scattered our gear around, quickly, as soon as we saw the hand-lettered note, "Welcome Buckeyes!"

The note became the little torch I used to try to get the furnace lit. The torch didn't work. Holding a Zippo lighter closer to the pilot only helped me to light my finger which fumbled for the thermocoupler. Kicking the furnace and swearing only produced temporary heat in one of us, plus a sore toe.

No problem, we decided. John would get the extra blanket. I'd get Paddy. Heck, I'd read "To Build a Fire." Didn't I know that a good dog can provide some warmth?

Halfway through the night, Paddy decided he'd rather have John and the extra blanket, and that's how things ended up. He never could take a floodlight in his eyes for long.

In the morning, the three of us, John, Paddy, and I, huddled around the open oven we were able to light. John and I each broke off a chunk of milk to chew with our cereal. Paddy gnawed at the block of water in his bowl.

But soon it was time for the hunt. Stepping into the tropical, 36-degree air, I strolled to the pickup, barely acknowledging the pitiful stares of the Ohioans, huddled together near the bait shop door, mom, dad, and two kids.

To say the least, all of this would have been lamentably forgettable had we enjoyed fine hunting and excellent fishing. Suffice it to say that John is considering mounting the only perch we landed and having it made into a tie-tack. And our only real contact with a woodcock went like this:

"See that, Tom?" John asked, pointing to a spot three feet in front of him, ten feet from me.

"Watcha' got, John?"

"See the woodcock?"

We spent the next ten minutes talking to the woodcock, offering it some lunch, exchanging photographs of the families. When the bird finally flushed, we each chased it with two shots—kind of like a salute. The bird flew back and circled us twice, trying to see what the commotion was. Paddy simply hung his head and made arrangements with his groomer for a brush cut so he could pass himself off as a dalmatian.

When we returned to the resort, the Ohioans looked dangerous. Yeah, sure. Like no one from Ohio has ever taken any of our secret hunting or fishing spots or pulled into a Big Boy in front of us and took the last parking spot.

As I prepared to check out, I kind of expected a discount.

"You know, we froze all last night because the furnace didn't work."

"Ehhh-yah. I guess you musta' requested the 'rustic suite'," he said, smiling out of context, or so I thought.

With a smack of her lips, Mrs. Fishscale leaned over our bill with her pencil working overtime.

"So we had to keep the oven lit and open in order to stay warm."

"You hear that, Ma? They was abusin' our appliances. Boys, them things ain't meant to be kept on all night. You ought to know better."

"Abuse charge?"

"Ehhh-yup!"

John's look told me to cease and desist. But I was long gone.

"And we couldn't wash the cereal and milk bits out of our bowls because there weren't any dish rags or towels."

"Aha!" he called out while Mrs. F. hunched over the counter and gleefully cackled from the ramifications of some secret her pencil had shared with her.

"But how do you expect us to clean the stuff if you don't give us the proper supplies?"

"Ya see the fine print?" Mrs. F. asked, pointing to a line of fuzz at the bottom of the list of rules. "It says, NO TOWELS PRO-VIDED."

She spoke in capital letters that were larger than what might have been scrawled on that sheet of paper.

"Even so, this is a kitchenette. Don't you even supply the linens for doing dishes?"

"Hey! You want fancy stuff like that, go to the Domino's Lodge they're buildin' down the road!" Mrs. F. advised.

At the bottom of the bill, she noted a $15 referral fee now owed to her by Domino's.

End of the Line

T he guns have been oiled, the clothes washed, and the gear stored. The relentless calendar, the same one that heralded the beginning, has now signaled the end of another hunting season. Just like that. It's so arbitrary, so definite.

It's just one more reminder of the end of the line.

I don't know. Maybe it was the early snow in September. Or all the funerals in October. Maybe all the dead deer on cars along the highway in November acted as the reminder that all life, indeed, ends in death. Even balanced by the joy of woodcock camp, the thrill of ducks landing amid the decoys, or the grocery shelves overflowing with bounty at Thanksgiving, the knowledge of the inevitable tragedy of life tends to dog one's spirit.

Especially when you realize that the line ends with the present generation.

I guess I'm thinking of Maureen and me, of Bandit, Libby, and Macbeth, of incomplete records, and of stories that, once completed, might never be told.

They say that two parents can usually produce offspring that exhibit the dominant traits of both. From Maureen would come intelligence, beauty, courtesy, grace, and hard-headedness. I would contribute the genes for an ability to read maps and to parallel park in no more than four swipes. But we'll never know.

Maureen's the seventh of fourteen children, has helped raised a few already, and is always ready to remind me, "There's no romance in dirty diapers." And me, well, I'm the kind of guy that thinks that mankind is headed for a suicide run with the way it treats the earth, and I can't stand the pain of thinking what type of world any child of mine would inherit, although she would be able to find her way through it with the road maps I'd leave behind.

Plus, if I face the mirror, swear on a Bible, and pledge honesty, I don't trust myself to be as good as my father was in his abbreviated tenure.

So, as I'm the only male from his large Irish-Catholic lineage who has taken a wife, it looks like the name stops here. Just like with Paddy.

Paddy's father Bandit sired several of the best grouse dogs in the state of Michigan, many through Libby. But both Bandit and Libby have died within the past year or so. And for medical reasons, I had to have Paddy neutered. So, even though he's got a couple of brothers and sisters left, for all practical purposes, Paddy is the end of his own line. He's had some wonderful days that make you wish you could bottle his genes and save them for an appropriate female. And to be fair, he's had his bad days, too.

The one day I anticipated for him, however, is the scourge of the testimony to his existence. For his first two years, I kept copious records of the hours we hunted together, the birds flushed, pointed, shot at, killed. Then one day, I didn't pay close attention, and we had arrived: I could honestly say that he had pointed so many birds I couldn't keep count. So I quit keeping the records.

Then, maybe because I noticed how completely writer Tom Huggler noted our hunts, I came to a realization. Though his beautiful setter Lady Macbeth died this year, he certainly must have the complete story on her, whether assembled in one spot or spread throughout his hunting notebooks. And I was doing Paddy a disservice by neglecting his records.

As a result, I started trying to keep track again. This season, Paddy and I saw sixty grouse and seventy-six woodcock, or thereabouts. Oh, yeah, and the covey of eight quail he pointed in the Thumb. At least, that's what I remembered to write down.

So now, the official records are officially inaccurate. But Paddy doesn't care. When we hunt, I can never get him to retrieve; he simply helps me find the downed bird and rushes off to find another. A professional dog, all he wants to do is to hunt, hunt, and hunt some more. It's in his blood; it's his passion.

It's too bad everyone doesn't have a passion like hunting, one which you are forced to abandon for most of the year. The importance of it would burn in your breast as violently as nature's golds and reds blaze in the bosom of her forests. You'd understand the essential need to experience, appreciate, and remember concurrently. You'd both revere and regret the short time allotted to you. You'd realize the futility of trying to clutch to your spirit that which will only be pried from your grasp in the end.

You'd have a realistic reference whenever you contemplate, as must we all, the end of the line.

The Hill

D eep in the woods far from the parking lot, I stood atop The Hill and thought of my Aunt Cora.

Well, actually, she was my father's aunt. And to be precise, I wasn't thinking of her as much as of her backyard. And if the truth be known, I wasn't too happy at the time.

Aunt Cora lives in Canada about an hour out of Windsor. She has a big white farm house, and up in the third story when I was six, some distant cousin who lived next door said she'd kiss me if I were Superman. Heck, even Maureen isn't that easy.

"I'm Superman."

Her luscious seven-year-old lips were moving in when I showed my true colors.

"No, I'm Clark Kent."

So she stepped away. Hey, that wasn't any good.

"Nah, I was just testing. I'm Superman."

Jelly legs.

"I'm Clark Kent."

"I'm Superman. . . ."

Kind of like Faye Dunaway in *Chinatown*.

Well, that nonsense could have persisted all day, had not the pounding waves of Lake Erie allured more than the thought of that girl's lips on mine. More treacherous, they were, too. To get to them, you had to face the annual crucible of The Steps.

You see, the back of my aunt's farm gave way to a cliff about a hundred feet straight down. To get to the lake, you had to climb down The Steps, all 116 of them. Each was only about a foot long and maybe six inches wide. And they were nailed into two long rails which ran down to the dock from the barn where the commercial fishing gear was kept. The last thirty steps were the worst. Through them, you'd see the rocks fifty feet below, licking their lips as you tested the swaying stairway. We never knew how old The Steps were. All we knew was that each summer they were a year older, a year closer to collapse.

I thought of The Steps as I paused atop The Hill along the cross-country ski trail in the local Metropark. I wondered if I could ski down it again, having successfully avoided it for the past three winters of poor snowfalls. And since we are told that "the earth abideth forever," I knew that of the two of us, The Hill was not the one who was three years closer to collapse.

"You go first," I told Maureen. "I don't want to get the snow too slick for you." The best lies to tell are the ones that sound as if you are watching out for the other person.

She zoomed away, leaving me to contemplate my fate.

The Hill has always given me trouble. I always slip out of control on it and fall down. The wind always stings my eyes. And one of us is three years older.

Five minutes after Maureen had finished the 15-second run, I kind of showed up, planning to keep quiet and return to the truck as quickly as I could with no further damage to my body or my pride. But Maureen would have none of that.

"Wow! That was a good hill," she beamed. "It wasn't bad at all. I could have taken it with my eyes closed."

"Mine were closed," I kind of mumbled.

"How come you've got snow on yourself, Tom? Did you fall?"

"No, I, uh, I was testing this jacket. You know, I pretend fell so I could see if it would keep the snow from going down my collar and up the waist."

"Did it?"

"No."

As she started striding away, Maureen said, "Did you notice those trees at the two curves? They have foam pads around them where they used to have bales of hay."

"The hay was softer . . . uh-oh!"

BRUMMPH!

"What was that, Tom?" She turned. "Did you fall again?"

"No, I'm just testing to see if it's still easy to get back up, you know, for when I fall down for real."

"Do you want some help?"

"No, I'm also testing this new technique for getting your skis untangled from behind your head."

"Why don't you let me help? Who do you think you are, Superman?"

Of course not. Superman gets kisses. Plus, he doesn't have to test to see if he can stand up before the snow seeps through his tights to his long johns.

The $1800 Woodcock

FEBRUARY 1990

L ike most marital arguments, or so we are told, this one was
punctuated with dollar signs.

It began with what I thought was an innocent enough question.

"How much of our grocery budget did you blow on dinner for my
mom?" I asked Maureen.

"Well, six dollars for the chicken fixings and about three for the
vegetables and coffee cream."

"What about dessert?"

"No money for dessert. We're on a budget, remember?"

"Whaddya' mean, no dessert? What kind of a dinner is this
going to be, anyway?"

"You don't need dessert. I'm preparing a healthful meal. I
want you to stay around for a long, long time," she said, fixing me
with that "I really care for you, Honey," grin.

"Why should I want to stick around? Especially if I can't have
any dessert? You'd get one fast enough if it were your father who
was coming to dinner. Ol' Chuckie Boy wouldn't set foot out of
Algonac if he thought the sweets would be missing. How's come you
shortchange my mom?"

"Me? You're the one who's a cheapskate whenever Charles
comes to eat. At least for your mom, I prepare regular food, even
though it costs us. All you ever give Dad are birds or fish you've
gotten."

"And those don't count, I suppose."

"No way. You go out, have fun, and get those birds for free."

Good. I had carefully lured her to this point in the argument. Stand back and watch the master at work.

"The birds don't cost me, eh?"

"No."

"Well, remember after Christmas when Chuckie came over for our wild game dinner? Let's talk about the woodcock."

"What about them?"

Now I had her. And so I began to compute. Had her compute, actually.

"Okay. Calca-pute this. Let's figure that one woodcock Tom Campbell and I chased all over the Thumb that one Saturday."

"All right."

"Here goes. I spent $11 on lunch meat, cheese, apple cider, chips, and all. I drove a total of 152 miles that day. Figure that at twenty cents a mile. After hunting, Tom bought us a couple of beers, six bucks. Then there was the ammunition expended."

"What's that supposed to mean?"

"How many shells we shot at that bird. Let's see, now, there was that one warning shot I fired. Then I missed those two shots, then the one when he scared me, then the two when he flew straight at me. That's six. I shoot premium loads at $8 a box. Tom shot once more when I was still crawling through the picker bush with my gun emptied. So mark him down for seven shots from a box that costs $6 for twenty-five. Now, add up all we spent that day. Oh! I forgot. Add in $3.48 for the candy bar and the Pepto-Bismol I had to get after the cider worked me over. Now, what do you get?"

Heh-heh! You could see the net tightening around her.

"Oh yeah. Add the $2.68 for the McDonald's burgers for Paddy on the way home, and the Big Mac for me. Whaddya' get?"

"Fifty-seven dollars and sixteen cents," she read from the calculator.

"Now. The breast we got from that 'cock weighed one-half ounce. Thirty-two half-ounces in a pound, figure the cost per pound."

Aha! I knew I had her right where I wanted as her eyes widened and her jaw dropped. Right where I wanted her.

"Tom, that bird cost us over $1800."

Okay. Now we're talking. How could she ever again accuse me of being a cheapskate?

"Tom, you know I'll never be able to create such an elegant meal for your mother. We'll just have to go to a restaurant."

"No, no. That's all right," I said. "She'll feel better eating here. She doesn't like dessert. Really."

"No, Dear. I insist. You take such good care of my father that I would feel absolutely inept as a daughter-in-law if I kept you from treating your mother just as well." Things had taken a turn that I hadn't scheduled.

"Well, I, uh, I guess I'd better change my clothes, then."

As I staggered toward the bedroom, she called after me:

"Better wear a tie."

Spit Take

T he most important thing I learned this summer was how to spit.

Twenty years ago, two themes that erupted in my scribblings were those of friendships and clowns.

This summer, I revisited all three: the poetry, the friendship, and the clowns.

About a dozen years ago, a fellow teacher, Tom Kroll, after losing his wife to cancer, uttered one of the most eloquent pieces of life philosophy I have ever absorbed: "It all boils down to human relationships." A simple truth.

If it sounds as if I'm talking in circles, well, I guess I am. "Cycles," to be precise.

It's impossible to feel any kind of a link with nature, the outdoors, without thinking of life in terms of cycles. Seasons. Repetition. Not boredom, mind you, but clearly identifiable patterns.

The same thing goes with human existence. It's a circle, the great mandala, the wheel of life. To think in linear terms, from beginning to end, is to eliminate the possibility of so much meaning and self-knowledge that come from understanding the cycles. To think in terms of cycles helps one to endure the tough times and to appreciate the good.

So what does this have to do with spitting? Oh yeah.

It starts with Oscar Bonavena, a heavyweight boxer from the mid-sixties to the mid-seventies. He fought Joe Frazier for the title, losing a unanimous decision. He was only knocked out once, that in the fifteenth round of a non-title bout against Ali who called Bonavena, "the toughest man I ever fought." I'm not a boxing fan, and anyway, it wasn't Bonavena's life that enthralled me. It was the manner of his death.

Bonavena was murdered in 1976, shot from a distance with a high-powered rifle as he was leaving a brothel near Reno, Nevada.

Heavy into irony and fate at the time, and considering myself a brooding, dark Irish poet, I couldn't let the opportunity for an allusion to Bonavena's fate escape my pen and yellow legal pad.

Recently, pulling out the old files of juvenile verse to verify to Maureen the accuracy of my memory of Bonavena's downfall, I was otherwise astounded to note that several poems dealt with clowns and sad faces and the masks we all wear.

The revelation came about after I had convinced our instructor at a Michigan State University summer course to let us out of our class early one day so we could go watch the clowns practice spit takes.

The clowns were attending a conference, and I had been torn between attending either their sessions or the ones for which I was enrolled and had paid. Until I ended up looking over those poems, however, I myself didn't understand why I had been so fascinated by them. But it was the cycle, you see.

We got a first-hand lesson in the fine art of spitting for the audience: "Try for a spray, not for a stream," the clowns were told.

The other topic I noticed in those early poems was "friendship." I had written poems about characters who'd save their friends, who'd always be true to them, and who would be betrayed by them.

In this way, too, the cycle came round.

Earlier this summer, I had been betrayed by someone who was supposed to be a friend. That had been bothering me. Yet, something straight-armed those feelings of betrayal to the sidelines the same day I learned to spit.

Norris, one of our buddies from woodcock hunting camp, told me when we got together in East Lansing that his medical exam that afternoon showed that he more than likely had liver cancer.

My stomach felt a void which somehow left neither room for joy at learning to spit nor irritation with a false friend.

The call to Maureen helped relieve the shock about Norris, but it didn't make the dizziness subside. Down to our group study room

I went, just for companionship.

One by one by one, people finished their work and headed for their rooms, till only Nancy and I were left.

And we talked.

Nancy, it turned out, had lost everything, quite literally except the clothes on her back, only a month earlier in the fires that had swept along the Au Sable River outside Grayling.

So utter was her loss that when she spoke of her dogs and cat that had perished, she could only refer to them as "the pets."

So we talked. Spoke of loss. Of dead dogs and of friends. Got teary eyed. We spoke of the need to be strong. Of the strength one derives through compassion.

Then we exchanged addresses.

Two weeks later, Norris phoned to say he had been misdiagnosed, only had fatty tissue on his liver.

At that moment, the ability to spit properly became ultimately important. With all the glee I felt as a child watching clowns at a circus, I took a mouthful and ran outside.

Through my smile, I sprayed a libation of thanks, for an upswing in the cycle and for those who would be friends.

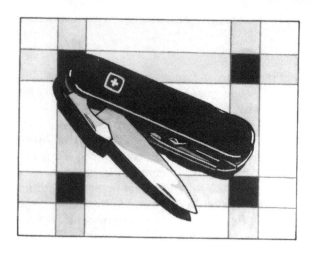

Old Friend

AUGUST 1990

I t's stuck with me longer than the girl who gave it to me, my Swiss Army knife. And that suits me just fine.

My old girlfriend was "thrifty," shall we say, at least when it came to buying me gifts or showing me affection. When I first beheld the knife, I thought she was once again showing how much she didn't care. But in the two decades the knife and I have since been pals, I've come to realize it is not a bargain basement gadget, but a finely engineered instrument. It's a model of simplicity, utility, and quality.

It's not a monstrous tool, not laden with things like a fish scaler or a wire cutter. It didn't come in a leather sheath. It slips lightly and comfortably into any pocket.

No hiker or fisherman decorates the red plastic grips on this knife, just the silver-white cross inside the like-colored square. The lanyard ring is a small, unobtrusive "S" hook. The knife is a spartan-like tool with only seven accessories: a single blade, nail file, flathead and phillips screwdrivers, can and bottle openers, and a pipe reamer. Since I don't smoke, the reamer has assumed various roles as a mini pry bar, shoelace unknotter, and sausage sticker in camp when I had forgotten a fork.

Since we met on Christmas 1970, the knife has flown, ridden, paddled, and hiked everywhere I have: Europe, more than half the States, the Bahamas, Canada, and all around Michigan.

The blade spread cheese on bread, both at the grave of William

Butler Yeats in Drumcliff, Ireland; and along the Montmorency River in Quebec.

It cleaned a trout from the Manistee River on that "I'll show you I'm not nervous" trip five days before my wedding. With all the elan of a cool, calm, and collected Royal Nonesuch, I had left behind the filet knife, tent, sleeping bag, all the rest of the camping gear and clothing as I breezed off. But not the Swiss Army knife.

The blade divided a chocolate-filled pastry for Maureen and me the first night of our honeymoon in Paris.

More recently, it sliced off a chunk of non-dairy creamer from the creamberg that had formed in the carton during the night of minus four degrees on John and my annual February float down the Au Sable.

The more I ruminate, the more jobs I tally for that blade: the rainbow trout from the Big Wood River in Idaho on Hemingway's birthday; the orange someone whipped at me in New Orleans during Mardi Gras; the blackberry stalks that had entangled the feathering of Paddy, my English setter, and held him like leg irons.

The bottle opener gladly stripped the caps off two cold bottles of beer that afternoon in Ely, Minnesota, when my father-in-law and I touched down after four days in the Boundary Waters. We weren't celebrating the end of the trip as much as our survival of the storm whose winds had kept us awake, alert, and on edge for twelve hours.

As I write this, I examine the knife more closely than I ever have. In the light, the grips show scratches and gouges, the sources of which I can only speculate. A small chunk of one grip has broken away, exposing metal where plastic should be. Despite my efforts at maintenance, grime accumulates in crannies that will never shine again.

I distrust the knife's implication and step to the mirror to check. My once thick, wavy locks have been usurped by my encroaching forehead, and there's skin where hair should be. Despite my efforts at creative combing, gray accumulates in clumps that will never see black again.

Would she remember us now, I muse. But who knows—maybe we wouldn't even recognize her.

I slip the knife into my pocket, hike to the basement, pull out the map book, and we ponder our next adventure.

A Treasure's Time Has Come

SEPTEMBER 1990

A mid the tables, chair, bookcases, lamps, paper stacks, computer, books, and ceramic mug, there are two homemade items in my office.

One has been in continuous service since 1968.

The other has been ready since 1984, but hasn't been pressed into use. Not until now.

The first is a piece of furniture that defies a simple attempt to name it. I guess you'd call it a telephone stand.

It's about four feet tall, and its top is just wide enough to hold an old style rotary phone and a pad of paper.

My father designed and built the telephone stand, the first project he created with the help of his brand new radial arm saw. The plywood out of which it is built has the tight grain and fine quality you got when you bought lumber back in 1968. The design is both elegant in its simplicity and functional in its execution.

Along with a fervor for honesty, a chronic bad back, a deer head mount I foolishly let go when my mother and I moved, and a few other items, the telephone stand is his legacy to me.

He died before the stand was completed.

A few weeks later, I assumed the job of finishing the telephone stand.

I sanded, stained, sanded, and applied a sealant. And for twenty-two years, I've known that the finish on the telephone stand is inferior to its construction.

Somewhere along the line, tossed by the storms of a Rhode Island autumn, I envisioned the perfect day afield: me, my father, and an Irish setter, marching together through a southern Michigan field in search of pheasants. Impossible, yes. Unattainable. Toastworthy if approximated.

When my mother remarried a man whose entire family enjoys the outdoors, I felt a step closer to perfection.

Though his children, some older than I, referred to my mother as "Mom," I always called him "Jim," could never use the word "Dad."

Near-perfect is better than nothing.

But Jim had a weak heart, could barely manage a few final deer hunts on his family's property in northeast Michigan.

Weak as it was, however, that was a heart of gold. And as much as I failed in my inability to refer to him as "Dad," he succeeded in loving me as a son.

The year before he died, he built me a present.

I had expressed interest in a gunner's box in a mail order catalogue, but I could not afford it.

So he built me one based on the original's measurements. That's the kind of guy he was.

Jim was in the hospital on my birthday but wanted to make the presentation to me himself. My mother had made a special trip to lug the thing down there before the birthday dinner at their home.

The box is crafted of fine mahogany finished with a coat of sealant. Inside, the box is divided into six compartments. Four are square, each big enough and deep enough to hold two boxes of shotgun shells. These are framed by an "L" formed by two separate, rectangular compartments.

Jim outfitted the box in brass: hinges, clasps, handle base, and corners.

I picked up some cotton batting and the velvet at a sewing shop. I set the cotton on appropriately-sized pieces of cardboard and wrapped it all in the velvet, making small pillows. A dozen various sized such cushions allowed me to pad the long part of the "L" compartment and one of the shell box areas.

The converted shell box compartment will hold my cup, a piece of Mullingar pewter straight from Ireland. It's decorated with an Irish setter. The other padded division is odd-sized, ill-equipped to hold anything other than a small, nearly square bottle of Old

Bushmills Irish whiskey.

Buckskin strips are nailed on the top edges of each of the remaining three shell box compartments. At ammo getting time, they can be used to raise the shell boxes from the compartments.

Having finished the box, I stuck it in my closet where it has remained all these years. Can't use it, I thought. It's too good. I just don't feel right. I need to preserve such a beautiful expression of someone's affection for me. But then again, he wanted me to use it, not enshrine it.

But things weren't right. No Dad. No Irish setter. No pheasants. Then again, things change.

I acquired an English setter, and grouse and woodcock became the birds of choice. But I still hunted alone.

Then, through my good fortune and the tolerance of a few new friends, things fairly well tumbled into place. And those golden days envisioned by an eighteen-year-old freshman at Brown University in Rhode Island became reality, albeit adjusted, for a thirty-eight-year-old at woodcock camp in Michigan's Upper Peninsula.

Fine companions, fine dogs, chasing fine birds. Fine meals. Fine friendship. Fine life. All worthy of a toast in camp.

I think it's time now to bring along another piece of sportsman's finery.

It will carry our chalice, a cup made of Mullingar pewter. And the libation, blackberry liqueur transported in an Old Bushmills bottle.

And I'll silently toast two men who won't be there.

Paddy

OCTOBER 1990

Y ou can take your golds, and stunning reds, and leaves ablaze with orange.

I'll take black and white.

No, I'm not rejecting October. Oh, this month of the hunt, this haunting month, this month of harvest. Oh, this month of sun-drenched days and two-blanket nights. Oh, October! This month that blesses with its bounty.

But my blessings are not found in the spectacle of color that highlights tour pamphlets and post cards. I'm blessed in October by black and white.

More precisely, I'm blessed by white with one big spot and several flecks of black. A few brown flecks, too, by the way.

I'm blessed by Paddy, my English setter.

Sure, Paddy and I hang around together the rest of the year, and that's all right and all. But every gene in his body screams for autumn. And it's true he and I enjoy hunting earlier in the season, through the late green and the fabulous blaze of color.

But it's only when the color fades that Paddy begins to glow.

The aspen leaves, once gold doubloons clutched by the trees, are now but counterfeit coins carelessly cast on the forest's floor and mottled with gray from moisture. The oak leaves that seemed majestic in their golds and burnt browns are now deposed from their thrones and scattered about, exiles. The bracken fern which only a month ago lived as a vibrant green is now withered, fallen, and has changed to dead forest floor brown.

I'm not expert enough to identify the other fallen leaves whose colors have bled into the ground to be absorbed by next year's crop. But it's enough to know that they've fallen.

For it's only when the leaves fall that the forest opens up for easier viewing. And the ability to watch Paddy work is the gift of late October.

And work he does! A professional dog, Paddy goes about his business in the only way he knows how: with an intensity and exuberance that leaves no room for nonsense.

He easily covers at least five times as much ground as the hunters do each day. You can see him test the air then double-check a scent that's confusing him. Once you get to recognize his moves, you kind of chuckle when his legs start churning, trying to catch up to that nose which is scouring the woods for scent.

The payoff comes when you are near birds, for he'll work close. Imagine being afield, with just enough sun to burn off the slight chill of the crisp October morning. The dog's bell gets louder and louder, and then the black-flecked ghost drifts into the picture. His head rocks back as if he's actually catching the scent of the bird he's about to point. The slight breeze stirs the white feathers on his legs and tail. A few confident steps, then a couple of rather tentative tip-toes in for a closer sniff. Then, WHAM! He snaps on a point that reminds you of all the old calendars you've found and paintings you've seen from the old *Field and Stream* covers.

My pal John Northrup witnessed Paddy's no-nonsense routine one day in the Thumb of Michigan. Paddy's expert day of bird pointing was complemented by John's expert shooting. Paddy would lead us to where the woodcock had fallen then immediately head out to find another bird. He pointed about a bird a minute for five minutes.

Yooper Jim Ekdahl credits Paddy for two of the most memorable upland moments he's experienced: Paddy, nose to beak with a woodcock for almost a full minute; and Paddy's locating a wounded grouse that had run about 150 yards from where a hunter had dropped it.

And just recently, Paddy reaffirmed his pedigree on his first hunt for wild pheasants. He outworked the Lab and Brittany who had been raised on rooster chasing. And while those dogs and hunters all stopped to yap with a pal who had passed by in his truck, Paddy refused to rest, choosing instead to vacuum through the tall, dead grass in the drainage ditch alongside the road. He roused a rooster from the grass that was so thick Paddy was basically hidden. That bird was my second of the day, my limit, but did not provide the highlight.

Working a hedgerow of a plowed field, Paddy suddenly slammed on point. My gun was empty, and Tom Lounsbury directed his son Josh to manuever into position to shoot. Like some grand puppeteer, I just sat back and watched the drama unfold: Josh, uncertain, kept glancing from his father to Paddy then back again, hoping for a clue. He began walking up behind Paddy who remained rock solid.

When the boy worked in closely enough, Paddy backed out, took a few steps down the hedgerow then curled back, kind of like running a fish hook pattern for a pass from a quarterback.

Thus pinned and rattled, the monstrous cock bird had no escape route other than to take to the air. With his single shot, Josh began celebrating his first bird. His father reveled in his son's success. And my joy was just as glorious as Paddy glanced long enough to insure that the Lab was on the retrieve, then trotted down the hedgerow in search of more scent.

Paddy was a gift from a friend, and thus he remains, but especially so in late October.

Seven years ago, I wrote "The Bond" which exposed my initial fear that Paddy and I would never forge that mystical link between dog and man.

I guess today I'm writing a piece which tells me I never should have worried.

The Modified Grand Slam

If you don't like my pulling burrs from your hair, you shouldn't have crawled through those thickets! Now, come out from under that desk and let me finish!"

I don't care how forcefully Maureen argued, I wasn't coming out.

"What are you laughing at?" I said to my English setter Paddy whom I had pushed aside. "You're next."

I usually get my hair cut three times a year: beginning of school, my birthday in March, and end of school. Now, in mid-November, at its best, my hair looks like Beethoven's after a grueling day; either that or the Heat-Miser in that one children's Christmas special from a few years ago.

Good thing my hair was long enough, or I really would have been in pain. The burrs were simply tangled in my long tresses. Imagine if I had gotten a nice, short, dignified cut. Those burrs would have dug in so close to my scalp Maureen would have had to shave out splotches, and I'd look as if I had ringworm.

"You know," she continued after coaxing me out with a dog biscuit. "I can always tell when it gets to be the end of the season. There are so many more burrs on the floor and in your. . . ."

"Owww!"

"Hair. Like this one. All this for just that one scrawny little birdie."

I stand above reproach, however. She doesn't realize that "scrawny" bird represents the first verified grand slam in Michigan that has been reported. Or that has been reported by me. Or that it's a modified grand slam, anway. Because I didn't get all the birds myself. And they weren't gotten on the same day, or even in the same year. But they were taken in the same area of the Thumb, so that must count for something, right?

Perhaps I should backtrack.

On the first Saturday of November 1988, my buddy John Northrup shot a pheasant and at least one each of a grouse and a woodcock.

"Wouldn't it be neat if a quail went up, John?" I said, reminding him that Sanilac County had been reopened for quail shooting. "That way, you could get a grand slam."

And he would have, too, but no quail took off.

This year, while I hunted alone, Paddy acted birdy but in a different way from the usual. That shouldn't be surprising because he was finding something we'd never encountered in the wild before. The first bird that flew took both my first shots. Then "Pffft! Pffft! Pffft!"

About seven more quail flushed while I watched, fumbling for more shells, hopping from foot to foot and hollering, "Wait a minute!"

Grouse and woodcock also flew that day, and if a pheasant had flushed, I would have been able to miss all three.

This is tricky shooting now. The variety of species to be bagged makes it very difficult on you. When the dog goes on point, you don't know what kind of bird will flush and scare you or how you're going to miss it.

Oh sure, the "Yeeeowww!" at the flush is always the same, but you don't know whether to prepare for a helicopter woodcock that might impale you, a thundering grouse that simply wants to cause cardiac arrest, a booming cock pheasant that might try to scratch you with his spurs, or now, the single quail that will dodge your two shots just before the entire covey explodes in your face.

The worst consideration is the fact that hen pheasants are illegal. This forces you to start shooting with your eyes open, of course, which also helps to lower your shooting percentage.

The explanation of the magnificence of the grand slam was lost on Maureen who mechanically went about her duties.

"Let's go, Paddy. You're next," she said, dragging him by his collar from under the desk after her usual ruse had failed.

He's too smart to fall for the dog biscuit routine.

Passing the Torch

I think it was the ducks that got me to think about the passing of the torch. Not the changing of the guard, mind you, not a simple cyclic rotation. But a transferal. From one to the other, forever. Utterly.

But it didn't help that the tape started playing "Girl from the North Country" by Bob Dylan and Johnny Cash the moment I began typing this. That was one of my favorite songs when I was eighteen. Eighteen . . . and I ponder.

Mild weather throughout December encouraged the ducks to hang around late into the season. About thirty of them lingered in the local pond until Christmas Eve. They seemed reluctant to leave.

Those are the ducks that won't return. Oh, some ducks will come back, we certainly hope. But to us, a duck is a duck. The fact remains, whether through predation, accident, weakness, illness, or old age, some of the individual birds were enjoying the pond for the last time. Just as some, to whom the torch had been passed, were only saying their first farewell.

Ecclesiastes: "One generation passeth away. . . ."

From the tape player blasts "Thunder Road" by Bruce Springsteen, my favorite when I was twenty-eight. Decades play out as neatly as cassette tapes. But there's no way to rewind the years.

Elmer Propst, father to my pal Tom, handed down his double-barreled shotgun to Tom's twin brother last fall. Its stock scratched in spots by corn stalks and worn smooth in others by Elmer's hand, it was a torch being passed by one who could no longer tend to the flame.

Elmer wanted to pass his deer rifle to Tom, but Tom refused. He's insisting on one more season, one more hunt, one more hour afield with his old man. If things go well, next November there will be a simple transfer, and then? Well, that's why Tom has two sons of his own.

Next from the tape comes a cut from Van Morrison's *Irish Heartbeat*, an album of mostly traditional songs he recorded with the Chieftains. At thirty-eight, I feel it stir tribal bonds within. Playing now, "Carrickfergus":

"My boyhood friends and my own relations," the song goes, "have all passed on like the melting snow."

Whenever Jim had invited me to join him hunting, or rather whenever I had taken full advantage of his reluctance to refuse me, I made it a point NOT to pay attention to the different routes we'd take to and from his favorite grouse coverts. After all, I didn't want to be a secret spot stealer.

Last year was different, but I was too dumb to realize it. Jim pointed out several coverts, many of which we didn't even hunt. Instead of taking one road in and another out of the woods, he just drove straight to the spots, then back to the highway, making the return easy if one were paying attention. He was acting like a tour guide, offering suggestions about helpful people in the town where his cabin is and where I had subsequently bought land.

Then at the end of the weekend, he dropped the bombshell. "I'm giving up grouse hunting," he said. Somehow I managed to suppress the "You can't!" that surged in my throat.

He had simply been preparing to give it up by passing along the torch to someone whom he had earlier imbued with the spark.

Oh, why do I punish myself so? Beethoven's First Movement from Symphony No. 5 in C Minor. The famous one with the "V for Victory" beginning they talked about in World War II. Come to think of it, I've always been laid low by the passion, the surging pulse Beethoven bled into this one. Maybe that's why it's a classic.

On March 9, Paddy and I share a birthday. One of us will be eight, the other forty. Both feeling the effects of age. Each unwilling to admit it.

The vet had said the time had come to start feeding Paddy "senior" dog food. After that, I looked differently at him. He can't get white in the muzzle, for his muzzle has always been white.

But there's the spare tire he's getting, and the willingness to lie around more and more, and the coughing. Just last night while looking at us in a mirror, I was sucker-punched by the utter realization that the day is approaching, perhaps not far off, when I will have my dog pried from my grasp.

And of course the ultimate utter realization that all things will thus be snatched.

Beethoven bleeds through the headset. I push the headset to my temples, and the notes seem to erupt from my very core, as if they were my idea.

The passion ignites; the flame is rekindled.

If I were King Lear, I'd rant with: "Blow winds, and crack your cheeks! Rage! Blow!"

Instead, I just clench the torch till my fingers cramp, and revel in its utter, if transitory, heat.

Final Cast

APRIL 1991

O n some celestial stream where the trout are always in season, John Voelker is sipping bourbon from an old tin cup and reveling in the effect of this ultimate yarn.

Like the waters of that stream, the name "John Voelker" might have silently slipped by America's fly fishermen when he died in March near his home in Ishpeming, in Michigan's Upper Peninsula. However, drifting around the bend with him was "Robert Traver," the pen name of the part-time author who initially shouted us to attention with the courtroom drama, *Anatomy of a Murder*.

The success Voelker achieved with that book allowed him to retire from the Michigan Supreme Court and to focus full-time on his writing and his trout fishing. His passion for each was evenly matched; he was a master, whether enticing a coy brook trout with his presentation of a dry fly or coaxing his "yarns" from his green felt tip marker onto a yellow legal pad.

Trout Magic, Trout Madness, Anatomy of a Fisherman, one or all of these Traver books of fishing stories usually find their ways onto the bookshelves fly fishermen reserve for "classics." It was Traver the author of fishing books who became the Messiah to legions of anglers. Had there been a vacancy in the Holy Trinity, they probably would have deified him.

Those who met Voelker spoke with the glowing eyes and animated voices of zealots who had been enraptured. They spoke of making pilgrimages to Voelker's camp at Frenchman's Pond.

Trying to capture the lilt of his voice, they often ended up speaking with a brogue, although Voelker was no more Irish than sauerkraut is.

They considered Voelker nothing less than a natural resource, as solid, steady, and lasting as the iron, the rivers, and the hills of his native Marquette County. Though they knew realistically his time was surely coming, they were nonetheless unprepared for its final approach.

One such disciple, Norris McDowell, editor, appropriately enough, of *Michigan Natural Resources Magazine*, deeply, deeply reveres John Voelker. Emphasizing the word "reveres," Norris explains, "I have trouble speaking of John in the past tense."

Norris considered Voelker to be nothing short of a treasure and, like a real friend, tried to share him with as many people as he could.

It was Norris who arranged for me to interview the high priest of fly fishermen, Robert Traver, in the spring of 1989.

But it was John Voelker the common man who showed up that day. At least that's what I thought at the time.

I took two high school students up with me to videotape the interview. That was the stipulation. Voelker would sit for the interview because it would provide the basis for an educational project. As a result of the nature of our visit, initial recollections play themselves out like mini-scenes viewed through a camera.

—John, in his trademark canvas fishing hat, blue and white T-shirt, khaki shirt, green sweater, and light corduroy pants, left pant leg hung up on top of his boot, hunting unsuccessfully for some morels. The man who would take three hours to "prowl"—his term—the ten miles from Ishpeming to his camp obviously hadn't taken enough time to inspect his shave that morning. As a younger man in a hurry might, he had missed a couple of spots. Likewise, he had skipped the center rear belt loop on his pants.

—Driving that Jeep Cherokee of his slowly, using main roads as little as possible, hugging—heck, *caressing*—the right shoulder until the driver's-side tires were barely on the pavement.

—Waving from his car to us following behind, pointing out things the non-observant would clearly miss: deer tracks; iron pellets at a railroad crossing, left there because they'd fallen from transport cars; the ruins of a farm house, the location of whose fruit cellar puzzles him; two trees on his property which had grown intertwined. In camp, from his chair he gave a guided tour of the various "treasures" he had salvaged from rummage sales. He said, "There are some curious things there. I love bargains, and I just couldn't resist the holy water font," pointing to the receptacle nailed to a tree overlooking the pond.

—Refusing to give up his fishing, hard-headed, an eighty-five-year-old man who installed a rope hand railing to help himself from his camp down to Frenchman's Pond. Chuckling, admitting that he often blessed himself from the holy water font, "sometimes for the wrong reasons."

—Decrying the spoiling of Michigan's Upper Peninsula by commercial interests while in the next breath denying he could/ should be considered as a voice to rally supporters of the cause. Doubting, really, that anyone would listen to him.

At one moment, he seemed to be giving us the Voelker public persona, the celebrity character showering us with his "fifty cent epigrams," the little, polished sayings that crop up in his writing and in other interviews. At times, he seemed a tired, old man whose limits were being tested by my incessant questions and the terribly hot May afternoon sun.

Flexing his wit, he parried my quick glance when he referred to a certain upland game bird as a "partridge." " 'Grouse,' I should say." Then, a thrust of his own and through pursed lips he added, "I sit corrected. . . . Don't grouse about my partridge."

He seemed a "wink-an-eye-at-you" buddy when he told this story: As a college student, he sold lingerie door to door. After a big sale at a brothel for which he collected a twenty-five percent de- posit—which just happened to be his commission—he was asked by the madam to reciprocate.

"We did business with you," she told him. "How about doing business with us?"

He muttered something about his religious upbringing, squirmed out of there, and relished telling how he was perhaps the only man who had done business in a brothel and left with more money than he had entered with.

Voelker seemed the benevolent grandfather when he bought the students and me a cold drink on our way back to Ishpeming at the end of a long day. And after producing copies of his famous "Testa- ment of a Fisherman," he patiently inscribed a card for each of us.

He loved to get out in the woods but rejected the possibility that he would have been happier had he lived in earlier times. "I also like television," he explained. With a little coaxing, he mentioned *Murder, She Wrote* as one of his favorites.

I did not visit Frenchman's Pond with the soul of a true believer. I was there to interview Voelker, not to make a pilgrimage. I had not been infused with the spirit beforehand. As a result, Voelker didn't seem to be wearing a halo to me.

He seemed to be an old guy in old clothes, just "prowling" around because he'd earned the right to. He dismissed any mention of his lasting effect and seemed unimpressed that he had millions of followers.

Maybe that was the key, I finally realized, months after meeting him. In an *On the Road* segment with Voelker, CBS newsman Charles Kuralt once said that a person is great to the degree that to encounter him is to be changed forever. If that is true, then Voelker, common as he pretended to be and despite his protests, was great.

Norris McDowell says, "John Voelker was an extraordinary man who loved ordinary things."

And now, while others mourn the loss of their high priest, I simply wonder.

I wonder how many more of us he fooled, like brook trout rising to an artificial fly, this extraordinary man, into thinking he was common.

Illuminations

MAY 1991

T houghts and concerns sparked by the year's first campfire:

Wonder why it feels so good just to sit there, tending to the fire as if nothing else is important. And nothing else is, not for the life of the flames, anyway. Maybe that's one reason we try so hard to keep them from becoming embers.

Like eternal moths we're drawn to fires. Perhaps we identify with fire's basic contradictions: it's a great destroyer while at the same time it provides for new growth; it's beautiful yet dangerous; the more it seems brilliantly alive, the closer it is to extinction; it is an important tool for survival, yet it provides enthralling entertainment; as a torch, it illuminates other things, and as a book it becomes a place to lose oneself.

Why am I such a magnet to the smoke? If there were two of us here, I'd run a fifty-fifty chance of attracting it. Alone, I'm stalked around the fire pit, the wind shifting directions 180 degrees just so the smoke can stuff my nose and soil my clothes. And wouldn't you know it, as soon as I turn from the flames, its escaping sparks fade into ashes. Before I can react, they drift onto and into things like my sandwich, my can of beer, and the jar of Miracle Whip I had left open in case I needed an emergency second sandwich. They do add a distinct texture to the food, though.

Sometimes, the flames, timidly wading into the darkness beyond the clearing, enhance the feeling of isolation. Thus deserted, you have an opportunity to eavesdrop on your own inner dialogue with no one to interrupt. Sometimes you'd be surprised with the things you learn.

"Whaddya' gonna' do with that pint of Wild Turkey?"

"What do you mean?"

"You've kept it, unopened, for fourteen years. So, you ever gonna' open it, or what?"

"Well, I'm saving it until I shoot a turkey."

"But I thought you'd decided this morning to give up turkey hunting."

"I did. But now I'm not so sure."

"Meaning...?"

"Well, it was only one bad day. And shooting a bird isn't the measure of success. I mean, look at all the neat stuff I would have missed today if I hadn't gotten into the woods an hour before daylight."

"You mean hearing that great horned owl hooting?"

"Yeah, plus, that one grouse that the turkey scared off his drumming log and the way he sneaked back. I got to see that and hear it."

"But look at the end results of all that. Especially after that turkey didn't gobble or cluck, and you couldn't tell if it were a hen or a tom. And while you hiked for three hours, you didn't hear a single gobbler. That's when you said you were too tired and too cold and you were going to give it up."

"Well, maybe I'll change my mind. I can always take a nap and get warmed up. Nice try, but I think I'll keep that bourbon bottle sealed shut for now."

"Have it your way. So, what time are we goin' out tomorrow morning?"

"I don't know. I was thinking about sleeping in and just going home."

"What! You'll never crack open that bourbon with this kind of an attitude. What's the deal?

"I'm kind of despondent."

"Over not hearing any gobblers?"

"No. There's something more. I . . . well . . . I don't like being up here alone anymore."

"Thanks a lot. What do you call me?"

"You're all right. But I mean, I get kind of bored with you."

"I can't believe I'm hearing this! You were the one who chose 'Solitary Man' as your CB handle back in the seventies. What gives?"

"That was more because I liked Neil Diamond then, you know, before he started wearing tuxedos and singing with Barbra Streisand and all."

"But I thought you hated people."

"I used to. Until I learned no one was forcing me to hang around with some of them. Now, I'm blessed to be able to know the nicest people a guy could ever hope to meet. Geez, that thought makes me happy. Kind of makes me sad, too."

"Very profound, Mr. Manic-depressive."

"Maybe you've got something there. It seems the times I get most forlorn are the times I start realizing how many things give me such joy, things that sooner or later will be pried from my grip."

"Like what?"

"Geez, where do I begin? Like woodcock camp in the U.P. Like acting in plays. Watching the woodcock dance in spring. Duck hunting in the marsh with Chuckie. Wonderful books like *Shoeless Joe*, *Blue Highways*, and *The Odyssey*. Watching Paddy work birds. Writing something that makes people laugh. Saturday morning coffee with my friend Joe at the Shamrock. L.L. Bean Maine Guide boots. Basketball. Cribbage. Quebec City. Maureen. . . ."

"Hey, pal! Slow down! Take a breath. I think something is sneaking up on you."

"What's that?"

"Middle age."

The fire diminishes. The flames begin to flicker. Soon will come the inevitable embers. Then, ashes.

The Comforts of Home

JULY 1991

My mother was never an outdoor loving person. My father died before nature shouted me to attention. In a way, however, each comes along with me on every camp-out, backpack trip, and river float that I take these days.

When my mother sold the house, lots of stuff just got packed and stashed. Once I was entrenched in my own home and with "stuff" spilling from the junk room into the basement proper, however, I had to start picking and choosing, keeping and tossing.

Casually cast in a box among the basketball trophies, the *Life* magazine from when Bobby Kennedy died, and the 1968 Detroit Tiger World Series mementos, there lay the lighter.

"Cad-o-Matic" says the stamped inscription. That was the name of the tool & die shop where my mom kept the books part-time back then. The lighter was a promotional item in the days when promotions were worth something. And right on the bottom where it belongs is the "Zippo" logo.

Everything on it is original equipment: flint, wick, cotton packing. I gave the wheel a spin and a spark appeared. So I bought some lighter fluid and let the lighter drink. And drink.

Then came the test. Flame!

Matches get wet too easily. Or their striking surfaces get too old and soft. Butane lighters can't stand up to a sneeze, let alone a breeze. Plus, keeping a butane lighter lit for any amount of time requires constant thumb pressure in an area that soon heats up beyond the lower limits of my pain threshold. And since they're disposable, butane lighters just don't transmit the feel of durablity that a fine piece of gear does. Not like my Zippo.

I can light the paper for a campfire in four or five spots from one spin of the wheel. Wind doesn't bother the obstinate flame; whenever called upon, it simply does its job without losing its focus. Any heat that does radiate from the closed lighter is the welcoming, comforting warmth offered by a hospitable old pal. The lighter provides an additional, inner glow as I think of my mother while slipping it back into my pocket.

Now the blanket is another story. It provides warmth as I wrap it round myself.

A big, fold out cardboard storage box held many sizes and colors of blankets, bedspreads, and sheets. A couple of sheets became camouflage for winter goose hunts. The spoiled setters, one Irish the other English, were bestowed with about a half dozen of the blankets over the years. But the best blanket is the one that was my father's.

He returned from World War II with this thick, olive green, wool piece of bedding. Remarkably, it shows no sign of being nearly fifty years old, and no moths have ever dined on its premises.

At first, I hesitate taking it from the house. What if something should happen to it, or worse yet, if it should get lost or stolen? It's one of the few tangible links I have left of my father who's been dead, now, for over twenty years.

I soon realize, however, that the bond will be served to better effect if I pack the blanket along on enjoyable trips rather than leave it stuffed among its moldering, less worthy companions.

And so, it comes along.

Around the campfire on winter trips, it becomes a robe when the wind wants to gnaw at my back. Inside the tent, I wrap my head and shoulders in it, my mummy style sleeping bag too small for my upper body. On the river it provides a nice pad and layer of insulation between the plastic seat and me.

Strangely enough, I've used it in summer, too. Waiting out storms, I'll often lie atop the nylon sleeping bag clad only in running shorts. I'll have the blanket over me and if I don't move around too much, I don't feel it pick me. And in some way I don't really understand, it seems to cool me, insulate me, against the heat trapped inside the tent.

The blanket is a comforting reminder of my father. In winter, I clutch it to myself with the intensity of hugs I could never give him. And in summer during storms, I benefit from an inexplicable force it still exerts over me and my well-being.

Though I might be on a solo trip, with the lighter and the blanket, I do not travel alone.

Autumn on the Wing

OCTOBER 1991

When talk turns to the woodcock, it's mostly a discussion of adaptation and evolution.

But I dig past the science, beyond things like the woodcock's prehensile beak and protective coloration. I examine the web that is memory, finding such things as a mishandled phone call, a Singing Nun, a phantom setter, revelation, and enchantment.

As a child, I had trouble understanding Uncle Packy's exact words: "Tell your dad da pat's is t'in but da peeperdoodle express just pulled inta town. See youse two tomorrow night, heh?"

But long distance calls, especially from Michigan's Upper Peninsula, were daunting then, so I dared not ask Packy to repeat.

When my dad returned from work I relayed the message as best I could.

"Dad! Uncle Packy called! He said the padding's tin but the peenerpoodle expresses the town!"

My father's smile faded as the disappointing message hit home, but he tried to recover.

"Oh, well. Even if there aren't any grouse, we can still have a good trip, ehh, son?"

I was too excited to figure out his meaning, what with this being my first hunt and with the prospect of seeing the pads of tin and the peenerpoodles.

On our ride north the next evening, my father deciphered Packy's message for me, pointing out that "padding's tin" meant the grouse—"pats"—were thin, or low in number, and "peenerpoodles" were peeperdoodles—woodcock, which he'd shoot if he had to but didn't really want to. I nodded, yawned, shifted in my seat, and drifted toward sleep.

But his disappointment gnawed at me. Obviously the woodcock ran a poor second to the ruffed grouse which my father often spent late summer evenings talking about on our front porch. But why?

"You want to see the bridge?"

As my father nudged me awake, the static from the fast fading radio station vied for dominance with the hit song, "Dominique," by the Singing Nun.

I remember scouring my eyes awake in time to see the bright lights above and the absolute dark below, so eerie. And the garbled French words only added to my disquieting sense of being suspended between the two peninsulas, neither of which could I see. I felt suddenly dizzy, confined, and restless.

Something else troubled, and I simply had to ask.

"We're going to hunt the woodcock then, Dad?"

"Why sure."

It didn't make sense.

"But what about spring?"

"Huh?"

"If you kill all the woodcock, there won't be any left to see their shadows so winter can end."

"No, no, son. You're thinking of wood*chuck*. Those are groundhogs. Wood*cock* are birds. Funny little things, too. If we can't find many grouse to chase, at least we can try our luck on the timber-doodles. That's another name for them, son."

So went my introduction to woodcock. A "funny little thing" to be pursued only if the grouse numbers were down. Known by goofy names, this "bog sucker" was not regarded with any degree of respect.

"Just look at 'em when they take off," Packy said the next day. "All dey do is go 'peep-peep' while dey 'doodle' tru de air. Geez, dem little fellas just give me da fits."

I had never heard my father refer to grouse as anything but "grouse," and at first I couldn't help sensing an undertone of scorn coming from him and Packy as they talked about woodcock. Once Packy had one in hand, however, things became clear.

By my early adulthood, filled with my father and Packy, I

echoed their traditional view of the woodcock.

"Nothing! Just another peeperdoodle giving me the fits!" I chuckled on more than one occasion after a feathered Artful Dodger had zigged and zagged through the aspen slashings, had hovered and dipped, had screwed me into the ground while picking my pocket of two more shells in the process.

In time, however, my companions and I grew apart, and for a long time I hunted alone.

By then, though, my book knowledge was starting to accumulate. Moreover, I had to admit that something other than academia was causing me to fall for this interesting little bird.

And in the field, one day, freed from the urging of others to "Hurry it up!" I finally took the time to appreciate the coloring of the bird. And the woodcock no longer seemed merely a lump of wet feathers to be stuffed away as quickly as possible. For the first time in my experience it became a deftly painted, precious creation—the pale, white dabs on the tail feathers; the soft, slate blue in the wings and back; the russet, the golden, the browns. Autumn on the wing.

Then came the day.

My father had never owned a hunting dog. Packy's collie ran afield with us but mostly for fun. I had learned to hunt woodcock by kicking them up where I could.

Finally, however, came a gift from a friend: a tri-colored English setter, a patch-eyed, coal-nosed, feather-tailed beauty whose every gene screamed, "Let's hunt!"

And that day in the alder tangles during our first season together, everything changed. As I stopped to wipe the condensation from my shooting glasses, the pup drifted like a specter into the scene. It tested the wind once, made a forty-five degree turn, took four more steps, then edged into a point, gradually. As if it knew it should stop but just wasn't quite sure why. The bird held. I watched. The dog pointed longer. For a moment, we became a trinity, focused and intense.

The bird was first to break the spell.

At this juncture of instincts, those of mine for predation yielded to those of the woodcock for survival.

Though the scene had erupted, it would be resurrected again and again. The bond among us three had become sanctified.

Nourished but not sated, I turned back to the books where I

found out about the woodcock's mating flight.

In spring, over open areas not far from autumn cover, the male woodcock puts on an elaborate courtship dance, triggered by a falling light intensity and lasting sometimes from dusk to dawn. Just like that, I became a two-season connoisseur.

And just like that, the bird that had begun to remind me of my own approaching autumn also began to baptize me into each new spring.

With time, new friends entered the picture, casual acquaintances at first. But soon we discovered our mutual infatuation with the woodcock.

This came to that, and artwork on one fellow's walls inspired "What ifs" and "How abouts." Talk came to plans, and before too much more time had escaped us, we were setting up an annual woodcock camp in the Upper Peninsula.

Those five days in October become both a fiesta and a communion.

From a distance, the camp resembles something traditionally reserved for deer hunters: sleep tents and pickup campers, cook tent and firewood. So, too, its sounds: joyful camaraderie fueled by an annual pilgrimage to the land that is holy.

But a closer look reveals subtle differences. Lightweight shirts and cotton duck brush pants supplant hunter's plaid wool. Fine, double-barreled shotguns replace high powered rifles. Closer still, the odor of wet, work-happy gun dogs mingles with the satisfying scent of equally soaked leather boots and woolen socks.

The camp cook—a true gourmet—prepares meals which surpass in quality anything most of us taste the rest of the year.

Woodcock camp is a time for generating experiences which immediately become savored as memories. Such impressions as the sweet sting of blackberry liqueur, the opening night's salvo, sipped from paper cups. Or the setter and woodcock, nose to nose for more than a minute in the lyrical, wet snow flurries until the woodcock loses his nerve. Or my "pointing," almost literally, woodcock for my companions, not once but twice, the afternoon when I carried no gun because my dog was resting in camp. Cribbage games played in the warmth of the cook tent after dishes are done. The four-course meal eaten from paper plates with plastic utensils in the pitch black pouring rain while the migrating sandhill cranes pinwheel overhead.

Sometimes the cookpot includes fresh game. Woodcock and the occasional grouse, if the woodcock are "t'in."

Here, in the land of Packy, I lie in my sleeping bag, stroke the setter next to me, and marvel at the thought: all this, each year, at the behest of a six-ounce bird.

A bird I once called "peenerpoodle."

Face-off at the Blue Wedgie

NOVEMBER 1991

B eware of maps drawn on napkins in bars.

There had been that invitation from my basketball pals, Tom and Bill Menard and Jay Andrews. They had already headed to their hunt camp, "The Three Kings," near Howell, for the November 15 opener .

Mark, the bartender at the Shamrock, had drawn me a map on a cocktail napkin which I foolishly used to wipe some beer foam from my chin. The foam smeared some of the writing.

By 10:30 Saturday morning when I finally got to a likely look-ing spot near Howell, the gate was not decorated with three kings of hearts as I had expected at this hunting camp.

Instead, the sign showed what looked to be a chunk of blue cheese.

I was intrigued enough to continue onto the property, following the drive until I came to a small cottage.

"May I help you?" a woman asked, stepping from the house.

She wore one of those black sweater-like things with a rabbit fur collar. Nice suede pants, just tight enough to keep you looking. And leather boots that nearly reached her knees. She kind of looked like a female "Highwayman" if you remember that poem by Alfred Noyes.

After a few moments' staring time, I answered.

"I was just wondering. What's the sign on your gate stand for?"

"The sign? Oh, you mean our emblem. It's a blue wedgie."

"A what?"

"This is the 'Blue Wedgie Camp.' Our camp game is Trivial Pursuit."

"This is a hunting camp?"

"Oh no, no! We're anti-hunting."

Turns out that during deer hunting season, Annie—that was her name—and several of her friends hold an annual anti-hunting camp from which they stage protests to let people know how utterly bestial, slobby, and uncaring hunters are.

"They want to kill anything they see," she informed me. "All they do is come out to get drunk, play poker, and destroy the environment."

She invited me in. Wine cooler bottles were strewn everywhere, and some had spilled on the white shag carpet.

At one table, a Pictionary game had been interrupted.

"We live hard and play hard here," Annie said. "Care for some breakfast?" she asked, popping a sausage link into her mouth which she kept open as she chewed. She reached for a croissant.

"We also have some ham patties and bacon, if you'd like."

"No thanks. But tell me, Annie, why do you protest hunters?"

"Because they're such pigs." She spoke with her mouth full. "They don't care anything about the animals they kill. Say, you want to stay for lunch? We're having some nice, fresh veal. One of my husband's clients is a meat wholesaler. He gets this stuff at a very good price. It's a taste bud delight, too."

"Uh, no thanks."

"Suit yourself. Whatever you don't eat will go to our two springer spaniels, Milli and Vanilli."

"But wait," I said. "I don't understand. What's the difference between the hunters killing deer and all the meat you eat?"

"Can't you see?" She whined a little, licking her fingers. "Hunters enjoy killing. Plus, I didn't kill any of this. It was dead before I bought it."

"But what difference does it make who kills it?"

"I think it's time for you to leave," she said, grabbing a chinchilla jacket from the front closet. "I have some protesting to do."

"But what about your jacket?" I protested myself.

"Ah, vanity of vanities. All things are vanity!"

"Et tu Brute?" (She wasn't the only one who could quote the

Bible.)

"But what's bad about someone hunting the animal he's going to eat?" I persisted.

"It's just . . . just . . . I don't like it. It's un-American!"

She said this, heading for her Saab while I scurried for the Grousemobile II.

I've got to get a new map.

Holly

DECEMBER 1991

I f Maureen had checked with me, I would have asked for a little
Holly for Christmas.

Not a sprig of holiday greenery, mind you; in that department, I
prefer mistletoe and its attendant benefits.

But a smaller, puppy-sized version of Tom Huggler's wonderful
yellow Labrador retriever.

Holly is eleven now. I've been acquainted with her for a little
more than four years, I think. But I really don't know her very
well. That's okay, for Tom himself only recently has begun to
appreciate her for who she is.

Admittedly a setter man—he sold possibly the best dog he'll
ever own, Reggie the Brittany spaniel, because "its tail wasn't long
enough"—Tom kind of always kept Holly around, just because she
was friendly, I guess.

"And that's Holly," he told me when we first met and I had
finished fawning over his two English setters. "She's a good ol'
camp dog."

And that's all I ever thought of her: sweet disposition, good old
hanging around dog. One who wouldn't pester you for handouts at
the dinner table. One who'd settle in appropriately around the
campfire at night, like a centerpiece with a cold nose.

Yet more than simple decoration, she's accompanied Tom on all
his hunting trips, the big ones to research the grouse and the quail
books, the small ones in his own backyard. And she's a fixture in

woodcock camp.

In camp, he'll loan her out to members of the group who are dogless while he sets a wicked pace with his pointing dog. He never worries that she'll bolt from them. Though she seems arthritic, and her light yellow muzzle has turned white, and the only black remaining on her nose is the edges closer to her face, once you put her down in bird country, she cavorts like a derby pup. And the guys she takes hunting always return with birds and tales of her expertise.

One afternoon, Tom and I being the only hunters who hadn't left for home, we set out on a short hunt. Two men, two setters, and a camp dog out for a fine afternoon. He shot his limit of woodcock, and I could have if I were a better shot. While the setters did a nice job holding the birds for us, it was Holly who made the tricky retrieves, who got the birds the setters either couldn't find or lost interest in.

This year in camp, on a blustery cold Saturday when Tom and I each had fled to camp to escape the freezing rains, Jerry, Randy, and Holly were the last to return. Two of them gushed over a dog's performance which provided them more birds than either had ever gotten, and they vowed that a yellow Lab was the dog of their desires. The third simply plopped from the van and stood at the door to Tom's tent until he unzipped it so she could then plop into his sleeping bag.

She's earned perks like this and like riding in the cab of his pickup while the other dog is caged in the back. Pretty good treatment for an old hanging around dog.

"It's funny," Tom recently said. "I put the setter up when I was out West and just hunted with Holly. The more I do that, the more she teaches me."

Like what?

"Like taking my time and appreciating what a great dog she is. I always thought of her as just a camp dog, but she is a heck of a hunter, too. Very thorough, methodical."

Me, I'm more capitalistic about it.

"Tom, you could be a millionaire."

"How's that?"

"If you could bottle Holly's personality and sell it to the guys to give to their dogs. She's just perfect. You couldn't ask for anything more."

"I know. I've really been lucky with her."

The luck became apparent a few months after he got her. Not a product of some high class kennel, Holly came from a farmer near Otisville where Tom used to live. The deal was he'd give Tom a Lab pup and Tom would reciprocate when his setter had pups.

The farmer soon hit hard times and simply asked Tom if he thought $75 was too much to pay for Holly, outright.

"Cripes, Tom!" I gushed when I heard that. "Jerry and Randy got seventy-five bucks' worth out of her that one afternoon alone."

Plus, just on me, Holly's lavished over $75 worth of kisses.

Whenever I see her, I drop to my knees to give her a big hug, and she licks my face as if it were smeared with beef gravy.

She does it year round.

And she doesn't need to be prompted by any mistletoe.

Good Times, on Ice

JANUARY 1992

Okay. Maybe it's true. Perhaps I'm ready to admit it. It's possible Maureen was right.

A "pack rat" she's called me time and again, while I maintain silence. I prefer to stockpile my huffs and sneers until such time as I need something she would have had me throw out a few days or years earlier. I savor those moments, for part of my self-appointed mission in life is to enlighten the woman.

But even I cannot deny she might have a point when I realize I have been creating a cache of old calendars, hunting licenses, and lesson plan books.

These have only been added to the fletchless arrows, leaking waders, and splintered canoe paddles, the fishing lures I'll never use, the three sets of camping cookware, the spare plates and glasses and linens for when we get a cabin. And the old birthday and St. Patrick's Day cards I've saved in boxes with old letters. Plus my essays from college. And every photograph and slide I've ever taken, those of fair quality and poor quality alike.

I survey my domain and admit reluctantly that my "stuff" has sprawled beyond our agreed upon bounds. I shudder as the words "clean up" escape my lips.

I must be very careful, for another person's trash might easily be part of my treasure.

An orange metal cannister that once held heavy duty hand soap catches my eye. I examine it much as Hamlet pondered the skull of

Yorick.

Like that sweet prince, I am somewhat bemused by the memories the relic stirs:

In the late 1950s, the "Whiz Soap" can held enough ice fishing tackle for a day on the ice: a few tear drop and Russian pimple lures, half dozen split shot, two small bobbers, and several bare hooks stored in a plastic tray with a sliding metal top—the kind in which replacement fuses for cars were once sold. The "Whiz" can belonged to my father.

Thirty-some years ago, building tradesmen in Detroit could figure on a winter lay-off as work slowed down. My father, a plumber skilled enough to fashion a lunch bucket handle of one-half inch copper tubing when the plastic one broke, masterfully constructed an ice shanty out of 1 by 2's and tar paper. At first freeze, he and his carpenter buddy would erect it over a hot spot for perch on Michigan's Lake St. Clair, part of the Great Lakes waterway. They'd use it during the week, stealing some time for themselves between infrequent side jobs and unemployment check day.

Most winter Saturdays, however, the soap can existed for me, and so did my dad. We'd throw two ice fishing rods into the car and head for the lake, about ten miles from our suburban home.

At some point on the drive from shore onto the ice, I'd inspect the lunch my mother had dutifully packed in my own lunch box, just like my father's but with the original handle intact. Usually the meal was predictable yet welcome: a bologna sandwich on white bread with plenty of mayonnaise, some potato chips, homemade chocolate chip cookies, and a thermos of hot chocolate. Dad's would be the same, except he'd have coffee.

Those Saturdays, my wardrobe was almost exclusively cotton based. In different thicknesses, cotton provided sweat socks, canvas sneakers to wear beneath my buckle boots, non-picky long johns, denim jeans, a flannel shirt, brown jersey gloves, and a hooded sweatshirt.

The shanty my father built provided the real warmth. If its small oil stove made things too hot, or if the smoke from my father's cigarettes got to me, I'd just step out for some clear air. About the time my eyes would adjust to the brightness, however, I'd be cold enough to step back inside where I'd be drawn to the muted halo that hovered over the rectangular hole in the floor of the shanty.

That screen held more potential than anything broadcast on our black and white Philco. And it always delivered, especially if I followed my father's lead and used a Russian pimple painted pearl white with a red dot.

We'd unwind the fishing line from around the two small pegs in the handle of each rod. Not long after the lures descended, if water conditions were favorable, we'd see the perch, first as it contemplated striking, and next as it launched itself toward the lure. Handlining, I'd give the fish a free ride to the surface, and "thump" it from the hook, as my father had taught me, by quickly bouncing it on the shanty's floor like a crumpling marionette. Using such a time saver, I'd quickly be sending the lure down for more attention.

Since those times, my ice fishing experiences haven't even had luster enough to pale in comparison.

Nowadays, childless myself, alone I hit Lake St. Clair or any inland lake I can drive to, even Saginaw Bay, a good two hours' drive away. Sometimes even a frozen river. I travel to wherever the reports say fishing has been hot. I randomly drop my lines, blindly angling for the lost magic of the experience.

I don't drive on the ice. Warm winters, hot water discharges from shoreline factories, and plain common sense make that a proposition whose risk I'm unwilling to take.

I walk, balancing an augur on my shoulder. Swinging from the augur's handle is a five-gallon plastic bucket filled with a commercially made ice fisherman's tackle box, two small fly fishing tins, four rods and two tip-ups, and two 35mm film cannisters with bait.

The tackle box holds a handful of split shot and a variety of minnow-shaped lures and hooks sized to challenge everything from bluegills to walleyes. The fly fishing tins contain a selection of tear drop and other oddly shaped lures as well as Russian pimples, all painted in colors that did not exist thirty years ago. The reels on the rods are loaded with line weights from one to six pound test.

The operant word these days is "portability," so I have to wear all my sources of heat. And I come layered in a variety of natural and manmade fibers: foam, goose down, polypropylene, wool, waterproof nylon, blends of wool and synthetics, and everything from boot liners to long johns made of the latest space-age super insulation. Furthermore, I have tried and returned three pairs of expensive boot systems in the last two years in an attempt to find something that will keep my toes happy for more than a half an hour.

I could buy a take-down shanty, I suppose, and use it to block the wind and most of the cold. But the nylon, aluminum, and particle board construction seems so flimsy when I think of how a shanty should be built. But there's little sense anymore in building a good shanty to leave on the ice. No more latching it shut, jumping in the car, and luxuriating in the security that all will be well upon your return. Thanks to both a mushrooming population from which human decency has leaked and the prospect for quick and easy getaways, a locked, permanent structure becomes an irresistible temptation for any dolt who can afford a snowmobile. Likewise, it looms as another potential loss for one who has trouble letting go of things.

No longer do I test the relative quickness with which perch attack bologna, white bread, or chocolate chips which drift their way. My cholesterol level and flirtations with the same heart disease that took my father have seen to that. Sorry, but a rice cake and some kind of a "lite" drink dispatched while standing with back to the wind fail to scream the palate to attention as much as rich hot chocolate and Mom's cookies savored in the warmth of the shanty and security of my father's presence.

Like so many other things with which I cannot seem to part, the "Whiz" can is a repository of more than just its contents.

Equilibrium in Spring

APRIL 1992

The momentum of the perfectly thrown basketball drew my hands past my chest and led me into a perfectly executed jump shot. The leather ball kissed the nylon net, sealing the perfect moment.

How little it takes to add balance to the universe.

How long did it take, from the time the energy surged through my body, greeted the ball at my fingertips, and encouraged me to drift back on defense with confidence? How long did it last—milliseconds on some cosmic scoreboard—this moment which set the world into equilibrium and reassured that all is well?

Perfect jump shots for me are rare, nearly nonexistent. Fortunately, I have other places and times to search for the blessings of balance. And spring is the time of the year to seek one which is much easier to predict and anticipate.

For spring is the time of the woodcock's annual mating dance, its prom, if you will, a floor show from above. One which reaffirms the fact that the ebb and flow of the seasons provide stability.

This year will be a bit more special, because the dance will both offer hope for the future and tighten some links to the past.

I often wonder if a person ends up cherishing a certain book or song or poem because it awakens him to some new thoughts which he finds appealing or because it articulates and verifies thoughts and concepts he's come up with on his own. At any rate, imagine your joy at finding someone who relates truths that cut to the essence of your spirit.

Imagine my joy upon realizing that some thoughts of Aldo Leopold verify what I've learned about the woodcock dance.

Anyone can find a likely spot that holds woodcock and from which to view their spring courtship dance. It's the male who performs this yeoman's task. Each night of spring, sometimes from as early as the first week of March through early June, he'll sneak from his hiding place in a thicket-rich lowland to his singing ground. That's basically what you look for: a fairly open field near low, wet areas. Even textbooks and wildlife biologists aren't any more helpful than that.

Once there, you listen. In fact, most of the time your ears must guide your eyes. The woodcock begins his performance as the sun is going down and he continues intermittently until it begins to rise. He begins with the first of his sounds, the "peent." It kind of sounds like he's giving you the raspberries or one "Beep!" from the Roadrunner.

The first time I heard one was in 1978. I was in the woods early to listen for turkey gobbling and I heard it. I had no idea what it was and no one to explain it to me.

In 1986, while conscientiously looking to find a spot from which to observe a woodcock dance, I heard it again. It didn't take long for me to equate it with the woodcock. Two summers later, I began hearing a similar sound in our suburban neighborhood at night and I was puzzled. Not long thereafter, from a hotel room in Des Moines, I heard that summer sound and observed a nighthawk dashing among the buildings. Mystery solved.

Only last month upon rereading Leopold's *A Sand County Almanac*, in the essay entitled "Sky Dance," I found his description of the woodcock's peent: "like the summer call of the nighthawk." Wham! A connection.

According to William G. Sheldon in *The Book of the American Woodcock*, the first peent occurs when the light intensity has dropped to between 5.0 and .02 foot-candles. Once the light drops further, the bird will begin his actual flights. The peents are purely prelude. He'll take off, with the same whistling wings as in autumn, and circle low over the field. He'll gradually gain altitude, he'll tighten his circle, and his whistling will become much more excited. Then, he'll change his tune to what I always called a "liquid trilling."

Leopold calls it a "liquid warble." Close enough! I am in league with an immortal on that call.

Once at the apex of his gyre, the bird will set his wings and freefall silently to the ground where he'll perform an encore, beginning with a shorter series of peents.

While trying to videotape all this a few years ago, I had to find a way to get more light hitting the camera. So I began situating myself on the eastern edge of the field; the fading rays of the sun would silhouette the bird if I were lucky.

Aldo says, "sit yourself under a bush to the east of the dance floor . . . watching against the sunset for the woodcock's arrival." Am I a happy guy, or what? Have I discovered the truth and then had it revealed to me?

Finally, I find my October hankerings now tempered by this New Year's celebration. A three-point basket could not please me any more than my finding my attitude reflected by Leopold's:

"No one would rather hunt woodcock in October than I, but since learning of the sky dance, I find myself calling one or two birds enough. I must be sure that, come April, there be no dearth of dancers in the sunset sky."

Maggie

MAY 1992

S he's "Maggie: A Girl of the Streets."

Her name came from my wife, Maureen; her subtitle, from a friend who had noticed a similarity between her and the girl in the story by Stephen Crane.

Like the title character in Crane's naturalistic novella, this Maggie was a waif. She was gaunt, sick, and badly in need of someone who'd love her. But that's really where the comparison ends.

For the girl in the story is last seen walking in a "gloomy district" as the greasy fat man, chuckling and leering and with body shaking "like that of a dead jelly fish," follows her to the wharf where the river streams by in "a deathly black hue." The last sounds she hears, Crane tells us, are the "varied sounds of life made joyous by distance," as they die away to a silence.

Our Maggie, on the other hand, entered our life only after our joy had died away in silence. Actually there was a sound, a moan; no, more like a sigh. It defined two meanings of the term "expire" as Paddy, our English setter, felt the effect of some drug whose name I can't pronounce. All I know is that the day after Christmas only a few seconds after the vet introduced it into Paddy's vein, it killed him and spared him any more anguish from the cancer.

A few weeks later, as we still suffered from our emotional blizzard, a meteorological one struck. I had just come in from clearing the driveway when our vet called to say someone had brought in a stray.

"And we can't get over it," the doctor said. "She looks just like Paddy. And you were the first ones we thought of, if you want her."

Well, I didn't want her; I wasn't finished missing Paddy. But the doctor called again that Saturday, and just to prove that I didn't want her, I drove down to take a look. She doesn't look just like Paddy. He had a patch over his eye. She doesn't. But she is a pretty little setter with a belton coat, sprinkled with black flecks like the snow beneath the feeder after the birds have tossed away the sunflower seed husks.

"Let me make a call to Maureen," I told the vet. "Just to see if she wants to come down and take a look."

To make a long story short, I drove eleven miles back home, returned with Maureen, she took one look, and we took the setter home, just to see how she'd work out. By Sunday afternoon, Maureen had declared the dog would stay—"even if she doesn't want to hunt"—and had baptized the dog "Maggie."

We've nurtured Maggie, with food, through various sicknesses, and with our love. And you can tell she just can't get enough. Oftentimes, she'll torpedo from the foot of the bed towards the head, burrow between us, and bask in our worship.

In Crane's story, Maggie has a terrible past which leads to her gloomy end. Our Maggie's past, however, is pure speculation. Maureen has decided Maggie is two years old. And since Paddy had been born on my birthday, Maureen has declared that Maggie's birthday is the same as hers, March 21. Also, as in the story, Maggie's fate was sealed after her encounter with the stranger. However, this Maggie, a perfect pet, had her fate sealed by a woman who only recently had learned the depth of her love for dogs and her need to lavish it on English setters.

As for me, my love is not as free-flowing. You see, Maggie has broken my heart. Twice.

The first time, a few weeks after we took her in, we were testing her hunting instinct at a local hunt club. My partner had wounded a flying pheasant, and Maggie just watched as it landed and started running away. I ran ahead of everyone else and shot it while it was running. The wind wasn't cold enough that day to cause the tears in my eyes as I lowered the gun and told myself, "Paddy would've been on that bird before its second toe hit the ground."

Hardhead that I am, I just simply decided to work with Maggie and to get her as excited as I could about running around afield with me. After all, even if she wouldn't point, four more legs churning the brush can only help when you're looking for birds.

Then, the next heartache. Just before Easter, the vet told us that Maggie had heartworm; she must've come to us with it. More of her past brought to light. The fact of the condition wasn't as bad as its prognosis: Treatment included four doses over a two-day period of an arsenic-based compound. Then because of the potential for blood clots, the dog can't run around for six months.

So, since Easter, I've sat here, looking deep into those setter-brown eyes, grieving for poor Paddy; for poor Maggie; and for myself because I won't have a hunting dog this year. You see, I don't hunt just to look for birds to shoot. I hunt to be part of a two-creature team. And once you've teamed up with your own dog, it simply isn't the same if you tag along with someone else and his.

Sometimes, I'll just lie in bed and feel miserable about all this. And I'll catch myself taking a Maggie-like stroll to some gloomy district in my mind, to a quay along a deathly black river.

But then the adoring eyes of the setter remind me of an obligation I've undertaken. And Maureen's, "Oh, you're such a pretty dog, Maggie," reminds me of the joy that only awaits my outstretched hand. And I'm reminded that I haven't been torpedoed since last night.

"Here Maggie! Up, girl!"

Reins of Terror

JUNE 1992

S wede Nelson got up, drew a tin of tobacco from the hip pocket of his blue jeans, took a pinch, and planted it between his cheek and gum.

"The problem, Tom," he said, "is that you didn't read our brochure carefully. It says right in there that we offer a 'high adventure,' you know."

"Yeah, yeah. But I thought 'high adventure' meant a 'wonderful experience in the hills.' I didn't know it meant 'a grueling and fatiguing equestrian roller coaster.' "

"Well, that's what it is. Why do you think we had you sign that waiver and offered you the hard hat?"

"You should've offered fleece-lined Levi's."

Imagine your discomfort after taking a six-hour hike through rugged territory in ill-fitting leather boots. Now, imagine that discomfort about three feet north, and you'll understand why I was eating dinner while lying on my stomach.

And worse than the fact that "Ol' Wadey" and his saddle had tattooed my backside during our trail ride, I had been branded a tinhorn from the outset.

"Wow! Those hills are really neat!" I exclaimed upon meeting Swede and assistant, Bob Wirtz. "They're so pretty and neat. Really cool!"

Tinhorn talk.

"Yep," said Bob as he rolled a cigarette with one hand. "That road kind of drops you right into pretty, dudn't it?"

Cowpoke talk.

I did nothing but enhance the tinhorn image all day. Like at lunch on the trail.

"How's come they call this place the Badlands, Swede?"

He just looked up from his ham sandwich with the same look of exasperation as he had when I had asked, "Say, Swede. How's come they call you Swede?"

Tinhorn questions.

These are the Badlands because, in most people's eyes, they're basically not good for anything. Here in the north unit of Theodore Roosevelt National Park, just south of Watford City, N.D., the Little Missouri River runs brown; so much sand flows in the water that even the tired horses refused to drink.

Some things grow, like sage, juniper, and a few scrub pine trees. Of this unit's 24,000 acres, seventy-five percent remains wilderness, basically not arable. Prairie dogs have erected a few towns and some bison roam. Here and there you might encounter some rattlesnakes, which real horsemen call "buzzworms."

These burningly bright Badlands are a place where experienced riders know enough to carry their own shade. And I did. (So don't tell me, Swede, that I didn't read the brochure.)

At the beginning of the trip, I had kind of moseyed from the car to the horses, tilting my Stetson "Gun Club" hat at just the proper angle for the desired effect. For years I had depended on its wide brim to protect my ears from my woeful dry fly casting and I had coaxed the downturned brim into an Indiana Jones attitude.

By lunchtime, however, with its brim now upturned, it looked as if it had been stolen from Larry Storch on *F Troop*. Wadey took a look at me and snorted. And he didn't like it when I hung the hat on his saddle horn for "atmosphere" in my photographs.

Tinhorn hat action.

This is a land of exhausting heat. So hot that the liquid margarine separated in the bottle and that Wadey groaned as he lugged me up the hills. It was so hot that when I sought relief by dousing myself, the water from my canteen was easily as warm as a comfortable shower. The heat provoked me to gasp a few lines from that classic western song:

"All day I face the barren waste without the taste of water. Cooool water!"

Tinhorn rhapsody.

This is a land of hills and gullies, of buttes and draws, but not many plateaus.

"Did I tell you that tonight's ride would be over mostly flatland?" asked Swede as we downed and upped through our umpteenth narrow gully on our after dinner sashay. "I must've made a mistake. Haw! Haw!"

I bit my tongue for, after all, he was my host. Plus, he had me. As the only vendors authorized to run trail rides through the north unit, Swede and his partner, Hamed Juma, were the only ones who could guide us back to civilization.

Besides, what could I say? My post-lunch comments had all been greeted with the same response: "Whatever you say, Mr. Storch. Haw! Haw!"

This is a land that was formed by and remains a slave to climate. With North Dakota skies nearly as big as those of Montana, the severity of an approaching storm can be discussed for an hour before it gets close enough to be felt. Also, the top layer of most of the trails, bentonite, came from volcanic ash thousands of years ago. Slick bentonite is treacherous for both horse and rider, so much so that wet clay remains the only condition which causes Nelson and Juma to reschedule trips.

The rain storms we saw never approached closer than about five miles before detouring. We were, however, treated to a North Dakota wind storm. Dust peppered our steaks and potatoes and, unlike those finicky, ungrateful horses at the Little Missouri River, I just closed my eyes and chewed.

Sure, the southern unit of the park, near Medora, includes a thirty-six mile scenic loop that the air-conditioned-padded-seat-comfort-of-their-car crowd finds so alluring. But the only way to get a true feel for the country and for the people who tried to tackle it is from the bottom up.

Tinhorns should remember, however, that they might be keeping their bottoms up for a day or two after the ride.

The Road Taken

JULY 1992

G iven a choice, I'd rather drive than fly.

This admission has less to do with any fear of air crashes than with the lingering memory of that rude French-Canadian who overflowed into my space and whose body odor assaulted me in massive waves during the 90-minute wait for take-off from Montreal on the last flight I took.

But the greater reason I prefer to drive is that you see more, sense more, get more of a feel for the places when you travel through instead of over them. Air travel emphasizes the destination. Travel by car also highlights the journey.

Consider several highlights from two recent journeys on which I drove more than 6,700 miles.

By the time Maureen and I got to Nashville, we were fully prepared, we told ourselves, to be amused by the hicks, both those who perform and those who enjoy country music. "How droll," we figured, "it will be."

How soon we were schooled.

The audience at the Grand Ol' Opry had set us straight long before the curtain ever rose. So did the young musicians reverently discussing "Mr. (Roy) Acuff" in the Shoney's restaurant in Music Row.

Yes, we eavesdropped. Good thing, too, for we learned. With a devotion and love that border on fervor, the fans come to Nashville.

Jeering the music is tantamount to making fun of another person's religion.

As we reconsidered, we discovered. There's a purity in country, long missing from other forms of music: purity of message, purity of intent, purity of adulation from fans. Maybe "purity" is too gushy; let's just say "wholesomeness."

Thus schooled and awakened, we sought the Mississippi River in places like New Orleans, Natchez and Vicksburg, then Memphis.

You really cannot comprehend or appreciate the history that flows through the Mississippi without getting close to the land that contains it. You can't get a feel for the vastness of that body of water until you travel for two days without running out of meandering shoreline. Finally you can't think of the Mississippi without recollecting places like the French Quarter of New Orleans, Port Gibson—the town too pretty for General Grant to burn, Vicksburg where the remains of the USS *Cairo* are displayed, and Graceland. This blue ribbon waterway wraps the geographic and cultural gift that is America.

The second trip, the one to North Dakota, gave me lots of time on the road to lose myself in my thoughts.

Just the other side of Flint, I was barreling along listening to the local country music station. Then they hit me, images from a song I now forget. But a couple of wholesome truths slapped me to attention and shouted to me what I tended to ignore: I had left the greatest part of my life at home, the part without which I am incomplete. And for the next ten days, I courted Maureen anew, long distance. Whoopee! What fun! The complete package—even those silly, chilly stomach flutters stirred—as if I were eighteen again. Eighteen. . . .

When I was eighteen, Bob Dylan released the album *Nashville Skyline*. My favorite song on it is "Girl from the North Country." And for twenty-three years, I had imagined a landscape which could serve as setting for the song.

I can't explain it as anything other than the joy of revelation when, along Wisconsin State Highway 29 and between Chippewa Falls and Wausau, THE SPOT appeared. I slowed down, fumbled for the tape, and transported myself through the country as the song transported me through time. The green, open spaces, the treeline in the distance, the white farm house, a single road: the exact images the song had engendered.

Other images stand out, well, just because they STAND OUT! Giant statues always catch my eye, not anything by Michelangelo, but something more along the lines of the giant Kirtland's warbler in Mio, something to attract the traveler. Do they work? Well, for me they do.

Several treats passed by on this trip: the brook trout and robin in Kalkaska, the running deer of Deer Acres just west of the Mackinac Bridge and its twin in Deerwood, Minnesota. Paul Bunyan stands guard in Manistique, and the snow skier drifts down a ramp outside Ironwood. We saw a giant cow in Peshtigo, Wisconsin, as well as one along I-94 outside an Indian relic store in North Dakota.

A fowling, we spotted a chicken in Marinette, Wisconsin; an iron loon across from the Pizza Hut in Fergus Falls, Minnesota; and a massive prairie chicken at the Rothsay, Minnesota, exit off I-94.

North Dakota held two more treats: the "world's biggest buffalo" at Jamestown, and a friendly golfer in Garrison.

My traveling companion Jerry Dennis of Traverse City and I noticed that golfer not long after dawn as we barreled into town to meet our fishing guide Keith Christianson for breakfast.

The night before, I had displayed my skill at letting the lady from the Lake Store in Pick City talk me into taking an ink pen with the store's phone number on it. Also the night before, we had proved our ineptitude at night fishing. Now, in the lull before proving the same in daylight, we searched for some way to impress him, to earn his confidence and respect. So we turned to the local wildlife.

"Say, what do you call those yellow-headed birds we've been seeing?" we asked. "The big ones about as big as blackbirds?"

"You mean yellow-headed blackbirds?"

Coincidentally, at that very moment, it became a matter of extreme importance for me to count the specks of pepper on my omelette.

The late scholar and mythologist Joseph Campbell said, "You can tell what's informing a society by what the tallest building is." Thus, the towering cathedrals of the Middle Ages and the political palaces of the eighteenth century towns. "And when you approach a modern city," he continued, "the tallest places are the office buildings, the center of economic life." In North Dakota, you see grain elevators.

But along one stretch of U.S. Highway 85 between Grassy Butte and Belfield, another structure stands alone. The exhausted tinhorn rushes past it toward a party store for a cold pop. But he figures, given the demographics of the state, that it is Lutheran.

The church stands there, a dab of white on an otherwise dull brown canvas. Brown, that is, except for the thick, comforting pines which protect the church on three sides and which offer relief from whatever scourge the west wind carries. Today is Sunday. The church is a magnet. The faithful are drawn from dwellings that are nowhere to be seen on the vast horizon.

The road is as straight as a runway.

But airplanes are the furthest thing from my mind.

Summer School

AUGUST 1992

The sun has been on the run for less than an hour. Can't waste time. I have to get up for summer school. My textbook is quite long. About two miles.

Quickly brewed coffee is usually morning's first friend, but today the calm, foggy pond beckons me outdoors. With an agreeable creak, the fiberglass solo canoe forms an immediate alliance with the pond's surface.

Likewise, the ash paddle and the water exchange a few low fives and quickly I am deep into the mist. The shoreline is never in doubt, so I don't need to chart my progress by anything as poetic as the wind in my face or the trail my paddle makes in the water.

After several lessons, however, I can chart another sort of progress: the various ways the pond and its supporting characters have opened up and have both welcomed and taught me.

Once, a hen mallard and her five juveniles saw me coming and glided away. No "hurry," but a lot of "wary." I had to consider. The first brood I had seen earlier in the year contained seven ducklings. Was this a second brood? Another hen? Or was it the same brood? Had a pike cut in during survival's incessant waltz?

Survival: Another hen mallard made quite a commotion, quacking in alarm to her brood. I looked up in time to see the bald eagle take a cursory glance, dive bomb them once, zoom in my direction, peel off about thirty yards away, attempt to score the catch of the day, then roost, haplessly I'm sure, in the pine tree across the pond.

Daily life: What could have attacked the bluegills we found at two different times with their tails and part of their backs gone? One was still alive, attracting attention from the sky and from below as he flipped among the lily pads.

Mystery: What a treat, the 19-inch smallmouth that hit a black plastic worm while I trolled in the canoe. It fought so hard and the canoe is so light, that I ended up getting pulled around by the monster fish I had hooked. Like Gregory Peck in *Moby Dick*. While reviving the bass, I noticed a fresh scar on its left cheek. It's tough to imagine a predator that would attack such a large fish. Disease?

Change, constant change: Each week, each day, the pond displays the cycle of things, nature's steady march, in much more obvious ways than a lake or big river will. Lily pads spurt where only a few days earlier there had been clear water. One day, white lillies will predominate; the next, yellow. The downy goslings that had tramped through our yard are now indistinguishable from their parents. And the juvenile ducks which just last week swam away from any threat, are now taking practice flights to different spots in the pond. Less obviously, the great blue heron tends to his work, as do the beavers, muskrats, and the occasional loon. The wood duck, only a few weeks ago just a hatchling tumbling from the box, now whistles her anxious cry as she catches sight of the canoe drifting by.

A small turtle swims by, just beyond arm's reach. "Gee," the thought occurs to me, "if I only had a net, I could have caught him and kept him as a pet." At that point I am overwhelmed with the knowledge that the zoo mentality must still fester somewhere within. The only note of hope is that almost immediately I realize that the whole pond is a zoo, and its exhibits are always changing.

Not only the animals and plants, but also the pond itself constantly changes. In fact, it is the child of change. Technically, the pond is a flooding. Like some skillful plastic surgeon, the dam half a mile downstream from us has transformed forever the identity and complexion of the river. Since it has flooded beyond its natural banks, the river covers hundreds of tree stumps in fairly shallow water. Consequently, the pond remains free of humongous outboard motors, water skiers, and jetboaters, while at the same time it lures my canoe.

The calm water of the morning and late evening invites me to try fly casting for some of the bluegills calmly slurping away in the lily pads. So flat is the water that I don't need to scan the sky for any bird action. If anything is in view, I'll see its reflection in plenty of time to look up. Daytime winds vary, offering new and challenging routes for drift fishing. Heavy rains thrash the surface of the pond, swamping the lily pads and leaving the patch of bullrushes standing alone, a defiant sentry.

Sometimes the pond offers so many lessons that two hours go by before I think of returning. On other days, the pond looks best from the dock where I sit with my coffee and listen to the bluegills kiss the bugs on the surface—kind of the opposite of our bobbing for apples.

With lessons like these, I feel no desire to return to the classroom.

Early Autumn Lullaby

SEPTEMBER 1992

D on't ask me why, but for the first time I can recall, I'm antici-
pating the sounds of bird hunting season more than the sights.

This all began a few weeks ago, when we were trying to get to
sleep on a particularly cool night at the cabin, October cool. Somewhere on the other side of our English setter Maggie, Maureen was
buried beneath the same pile of blankets that were supposed to be
covering me.

When Maggie decided to join us, however, she had struck
without warning. The result was that I couldn't protect my share of
the blankets, which became her cradle, and the part of me that
wasn't facing the middle of the bed was left unprotected, shivering
in the night.

And I lay there thinking. And listening.

The wind-up clock on the night stand talked to me, tick-tick,
tick-tick, tick-tick. A reminder of simple things not long past, the
clock also became a harbinger, heralding the fact that soon the days
for the hunt would arrive.

How like the clock I am the night before the year's first hunt.
I'm wound as tightly: my internal alarm will sound a half-dozen
times before the mechanical one ever shakes itself awake. In years
past, my old setter Paddy would have paced, affording neither of us
any appreciable sleep. This year, Maggie, recovering from heartworm, can't hunt, so she snoozes, and the puppy has no idea of how
excited she is supposed to be at this time of the year. So, I will fret

for the lot of us.

But I will take the puppy to the field for her no-pressure season. And when once I would not have hunted a dog without having him wear an electronic beeper, I think that Lucy will spend most of this year sporting a little brass bell. Sure the beepers are most helpful when you're trying to locate a dog on point, but the bell sounds, well, it just sounds classic and placid. Simple, low-tech, almost reassuring.

Just a bit of technology will trigger the tubular "thwooone" when the auto ejectors on my over and under launch the husk of the single shell I've just fired at the woodcock I'm sure has fallen. To be sure, I hope others will hear my "Dead bird, Lucy! Fetch here! What a good girl!" I hope. I hope.

One constant Lucy will hear in camp next week is the friendly hiss of a Coleman lantern. We take a big breakfast in the dark and return after dusk, so the Coleman's call will be part of the daily sound track. So will the pop and sizzle of the camp cook's magic in the Durango cooker. And if she's lucky, Lucy will share in the performance of the migrating sandhill cranes, croaking like a dozen rusty old gates pinwheeling across the starlit sky.

The campfire will be different from at the cabin. In camp, we'll need a conflagration for group warmth and illumination. The most pleasant sound from the fireplace at the cabin, however, is the medium-sized fire as it settles in after blazing, getting ready to burn itself out. Neither a crackle nor a snapping, it spits out more of a crinkle. Just the heartbeat of the fire as it does its job. All else is silent.

While the cabin does have conveniences like a television, nothing replaces the good old conversation that gets stirred up after a full day, a round of drinks and a round of cribbage, the social milieu for such talk.

And when work schedules force us to abandon the north, Maureen and I unwind around the dashboard and steering wheel as we head south. It has evolved into a bit of a ritual in itself. She'll allow me to doze no more than three times before she takes over the driving chores. I can never relax because the passenger seat is too small. So, if we don't have a newspaper, I soon get bored. The outward sign of my boredom is always the same: I experiment with the various configurations I can imagine for draping my red bandana over and around my head. My all-time favorite is the "Ghost of Jacob Marley" look which calls for the hanky to be wrapped beneath my chin and tied at the top of my head.

Once the bandana tricks get old, or as soon as Maureen can no longer ignore me—whichever comes first—something might spur the conversation. Like a white pickup with Ohio plates that flashes its brights for Maureen to move aside and passes us going better than 85 mph.

"Don't you wish sometimes that you could be Superman for just a little while?" I ask.

"Or Carrie," she says, remembering the telekinetic Stephen King character.

There follow a few minutes of cogitation during which Maureen decides, "I wouldn't do anything to hurt the guy. Just make him wet his pants or something that would slow him down." And I aver as to how I'd like to fly underneath him and hold his truck in the air so he couldn't understand why his motor was running but he wasn't moving.

When I really get bored, I start singing, more sounds of the season. After a particularly effective duet of "Shiloh" with Neil Diamond, I once asked Maureen, "Say, what kind of song styling is my voice best suited for? You know, Sinatra, show tunes, rock, country?"

"What music is best for your voice?" she asked.

"Yeah."

"Instrumentals."

That comment still burned as I lay there, unable to sleep, the room lit by the moon. But then I tuned into a collaboration of sounds I could never before associate with the season.

The puppy snored in her cage. Maggie gave a sigh now and then. Maureen's rhythmic breathing provided a counterbeat to the clock. The cabin creaked agreeably.

Sometimes life becomes symphonic.

At Home, Alone

As Maureen packed for a week's visit to her aunt's winter home in Florida, I wrestled, unsuccessfully, with a goofy grin.

"Tom, you aren't planning on being a 'free man in Paris' while I'm gone, like you were last year, are you?"

Actually I was planning on it. But even now a year later, Maureen insists the house still smells like burnt popcorn. And she has never believed that the fire marshall told me that lots of people panic in the same manner when the smoke alarm goes off. So I told her the truth.

"No."

To sell that notion, I'll mope around a little and act the role, but as soon as she and her father pull out the driveway, I'm gonna' be a guy. My own man. Take nothin' from nobody. Free man. Yeah.

I'll do guy things. Drink milk straight from the jug. Walk around in my underwear and leave it on the dresser if I feel like it.

I'll do other guy things like leaving the toilet seat up the entire week and cranking up the stereo. Yeah. Tom Waits, Springsteen, some Kentucky Headhunters, and Van Morrison. All those guy tunes she makes me wear a headset for while she's at home. Yeah.

I'll go to guy places. I might buy some strawberries, some shortcake, and unload an entire can of whipping cream on one serving. To conserve dishes, dish water, soap, rinse water, and energy, I'll use one plate the entire week. I'll watch World War II documentaries on the Arts & Entertainment station. Free man.

—Monday night's phone call:

"Hi, Tom!" said Maureen. "I just wanted to call to let you know we got in all right. How's everything?"

"Good."

"Tom, speak up. I can't hear you. Do you have the stereo turned up?"

"Oh, yeah. I guess I do. Here, let me take care of that. (Heh! Heh!)"

This is the spot where I always turn the music up louder than it was, then return it to its original spot.

"Tom, are you blasting out the neighborhood with show tunes again?"

"Well, not real show tunes. 'Jacques Brel . . .' is more like a revue; it's not like a musical or anything. It's guy stuff."

"Well, just be careful. Remember what happened last time when the neighbors heard you singing 'Some Enchanted Evening.' Well, I'd better go. I just wanted to check in. Oh. Don't forget to leave the toilet seat up so the girls can get their water."

—Tuesday night's call:

"Hi, Tom. What's new?"

"There's lipstick prints on mouth of the milk jug."

"Oh, I forgot to tell you. I copied your idea. That sure saves a lot of time for me in the morning. (Heh! Heh!)."

"That's not funny."

"What have you been doing?" she asked. "Did you go ice fishing with Propster this week?"

"I was supposed to, but I decided that I didn't want to, so I made up my own mind not to go with him. Nobody told me I couldn't; I just decided."

"How did Propst do?"

"He got a bucketful of perch, plus two nice walleyes."

"Too bad you didn't want to go. Bye-bye!"

No calls on Wednesday or Thursday.

—Friday:

"Hi, Aunt Franny? This is Tom. Can I speak to Maureen . . . sorry, may I please speak to her?"

"Hi, Tom!" said Maureen.

"The dogs miss you and wanted me to call."

"What's wrong?"

"Nothing."

"Have you been taking care of things all right?" she asked.

"Well, I've fed the girls everyday. Plus watered your plants. Plus the driveway wasn't shoveled by the time I got home. So I did that. Yesterday, I tried driving out to the fishing show at the Palace, but the snow was too bad, so I turned back and came home. So I'll go there tomorrow before hitting Outdoorama. Oh yeah. I got bored and washed dishes."

"You actually used more than one plate this week?"

"No. But I used two glasses."

"Why?"

"I used the first one to water your plants, and it kind of brushed against the poinsettia, and I heard that they were poisonous, so I didn't want to take any chances.

"Have you been eating properly?"

"Well, kind of."

"What does that mean? I went to a lot of trouble preparing those meals that I left in the refrigerator for you."

"Yeah," I said. "But your list only told me what to eat for three days. I had to figure stuff out on my own for the last two days."

"Tom! Those meals were supposed to last six days! Did you eat them all in three?"

"I guess so. It was gone, so I went looking in the pantry for something."

"So what did you have for dinner yesterday?"

"Marshmallows."

"That's it?"

"Grits."

"Good grief." Then she added, "So what did you . . . prepare tonight?"

"I found a couple tubes of cheese product left over from that sampler you got for Christmas."

"Anything else?"

"No."

"Tom, you're the world's worst liar. So what else did you have?"

"How do you get a burnt popcorn stain out of the popper?"

"Tom, you *didn't*! Not again!"

"But it was only in the microwave for twelve minutes this time."

"Fine. Now, I hate to ask this, but what are you going to do for dinner tomorrow night?

"I'm going to a restaurant. The fire marshall's buying."

Hymns and Libations

MAY 1993

U nlike in books and movies, meaning in our lives rarely surfaces in wondrous moments of heightened adventure or
passion. More often than not, the significant lurks in the common-
place; life's poetry, in the prosaic.

And quite often these episodes gain additional status because of
the special components associated with them.

Take music, for example. So many special if not supreme
moments are enhanced by the melodies that unwaveringly accom-
pany them.

In the summer of 1976, my buddy Danny and I spent the
bicentennial in the Upper Peninsula with Danny's brother and his
family. This trip was the first date with a place which I have since
grown to love. And it was the only time that Dan, two days my
younger, and I ever got together for an extended trip.

That summer, the Beatles re-released, "Got to Get You into My
Life," and the tune tracked us from radio station to radio station
throughout the state. As we pulled up to a bar in Indian River, as
we rolled into sunrise in Munising, as we stopped in L'Anse for a
cinnamon roll, the song etched its way into the trip.

Between fishing and drinking excursions, glancing at the TV's,
we caught a glimpse of the long ships pulling into New York. We
got Danny's brother Ted in trouble by taking him to a topless bar on
the way to Lake Linden. We made a quick side trip to the national
park that Danny always called "*Island* Royale." And after the

Fourth of July parade in downtown Houghton, I must have made some kind of a comment to a local girl who responded in her strongest Finnish accent, "What do ya tink I am, a whooore?" And at every turn in the long and winding road, we encountered the Beatles.

Of course, John Lennon was still alive then. So was Danny.

Years later, another trip's theme song developed as my father-in-law Charles, my brother-in-law Jim, Jim's best friend Web, and I met up for our first "Moses" fishing trip at the Weber family camp, "Dismusbedaplace," outside of Michigamme, also in the U.P.

Bryan Adams' "Summer of '69" battled Bruce Springsteen's "Glory Days" for the honor of theme song for the trip. Each got equal air play, or so it seemed, until the third day of the trip, when Jimmer, Web, and I, all avowed Springsteen junkies, pronounced "Glory Days" to be the champion. Charles didn't vote, opting instead to complain about "bang-bang" music of all types.

That Moses trip hadn't been dedicated to the Lawgiver beforehand, not until the night of the rainstorm and no bites, when Jim and I thought we saw a monster fish swimming the shallows and lashing out unsuccessfully at our lures. It crashed at a Rapala at the same moment lightning flashed—like the climactic moment in the movie *The Natural* just before Robert Redford swats his home run.

Thus imbued, Jimmer and I raced back, our paddles never pausing, our eyes never blinking, and interrupted Web and Charles at their cribbage game.

Long past midnight, after the storm had moved along, Web and I paddled to the opposite end of the lake, and on my first cast into the darkness, "Spaloonge!" the shadowy vision protested the lure but did not hook himself.

Thus inspired, we christened the beast, "Moses," for he had brought us the true word and had pointed the way.

The next day, we opted to mess around at some insignificant back country lakes until dark when we would return to stalk our swimming prophet.

Upon our return to camp, who should we encounter sitting there, burning the firewood we had gathered, eating our steaks, and showing off a couple of nice walleyes on his stringer but Web's brother, Karl.

"Hey! Did youse guys see the otter splashing out there?" Karl asked. "Boy, he sure makes a fuss after those Rapalas, eh?"

To top it off, he was drinking our beer.

Less detailed but memorable nonetheless was the June morning I drove my little car back to a lake at the Lapeer Game Area to try some fly rodding for bluegill from a float tube. As I rolled quietly down the two-track to the lake, a movement from Copland's *Appalachian Spring* manifested itself on the radio. Like a stage curtain, the mist slowly lifted from the small lake. The music pleasantly commingled with the notes of some nearby birds. A true symphony. Never before had a moment seemed so blessed by its own personalized theme music.

Same thing happened on an early Saturday one October. Rushing to an appointed rendezvous for some pheasant chasing in Michigan's Thumb, I rounded a curve and headed eastward, just as the sun lifted a lazy eyelid on the day. And just as the "Sunrise" movement from Grofé's *Grand Canyon Suite* reached its crescendo on the radio. It doesn't have to be church music to achieve spirituality.

Similarly, not long after dawn one Sunday, Jerry Dennis and I were hot-footing it out of Des Moines. The writers' conference had left us worn out, yet invigorated, like basketball players after a couple of hours of scrimmages. Just before we hit the interstate, Jerry had gotten each of us a cardboard cup of convenience store coffee while I had fiddled with the radio. We were feeling great about everything that had happened in the previous week, great about the town, great about the fact that we were bounding home; nothing could enhance the moment. So we thought. Then with the state capitol still visible in our mirrors, near an exit off I-80, during the melancholy strains of Pachelbel's *Canon*, we noticed a whitetailed deer raise its head from the grass, bid adieu with a twitch of its tail, turn and leap over the wire fence, and head toward the woods.

Music sometimes approaches the mystical. The first time I heard Ted Nugent's "Fred Bear" song, I was barreling up M-65 just south of Glennie. When Ted sang the part about the big buck stepping from the mist, I glanced at the tree line that bisected the field along the road. From an opening, right on cue, stepped a whitetail.

Probably no moment has ever been better orchestrated than that early November evening as I returned from pheasant hunting

in the Thumb. Paddy had done a wonderful job on his first expo-
sure to wild pheasants, including handling a big cock bird so
expertly that the twelve-year-old boy with us got his first clean shot
at what proved to be his first bird killed. The day had been cool and
sunny, with just enough of a breeze to make for good scenting
conditions and to cause leaves to tumble down main street in Cass
City like the trick-or-treaters had a few days earlier.

On the way home, south of Almont, I first detected the fra-
grance. Rolling down the window, I tilted my head toward the
hunter's moon, inhaled deeply, and reveled in the hearty bouquet of
apples ready for the harvest.

At that moment, something prompted me to twist the knob.
And at that moment, Van Morrison's "Moondance" haunted from
the radio.

As does music, so too do certain beverages add savor to special
scenes.

One night, near Ketchum, Idaho, Jerry Pleysier introduced me
to his favorite drink, a White Russian. A mule deer angled down
the ridge and set up a watching position just beyond our campsite
as we mixed a second pitcher of the creamy Cossack concoction.

Though blessed by the deer, this moment could never be sacred,
we decided, ever. For pristine as the setting was, it lacked two
components that have been forever and utterly pried from our list of
possibilities.

"Gentlemen, I give you our fathers," I toasted, and Jerry lifted
his glass. I don't know if he listened to the rest of my babbling, but
the campfire did and would never forget.

And if it took a booze-induced vision on a mountainside in Idaho
for me to understand that I'd never try to have children because I
could never be as good a father as mine was, then so it did.

Back in Michigan at Hubbard Lake a few years later, I ordered
the Canadian Club and ginger ale. It's not a drink I usually order.
And maybe it sounds a little classy for me. But I was feeling classy
that night. Along with my pal Glenn Patterson, I celebrated
something classic: Paddy's first point of a grouse, October 20, 1984.

And a Pepsi Cola never tasted better than it did one midnight, a
few minutes after I had left the Manistee River with that wonderful
brown trout in tow. Several trout of moderate size had obliged me
during the mayfly hatch that night, though I had deliberately kept
the creel empty.

I had begun to wade to my crawl out spot when he revealed himself with his first slurps.

What could I do? He was blocking my path. So for the better part of an hour I presented the fly, time after time after time, until he finally hit.

Yes!

I had promised myself I'd keep a fish if it were worthy enough of the baking plank we had bought as a gift for my step-father Jim. Coupled with the fish, the plank would be a special gift from Maureen and me as we drifted home for Father's Day.

A few Octobers later, the four of us—Norris, Jim, Jerry, and I—received a special blessing from the goddess of the hunt as we discovered a U.P. woodcock covert we now respectfully refer to as "The Place Between Two Rivers." Special, nearly mystical events transpired there. Wishing to bask in their warmth among ourselves before the obligatory recollection of events at dinner in camp, we detoured to a bar in Republic. Blackberry liqueur was our libation of choice. After a few, we stepped merrily into the street where Republic's only traffic light had been given the night off.

Henceforth, the blackberry liqueur became our camp's traditional opening salvo and, together with the homemade Bailey's Irish Cream, it comprises my major contribution to the camp's larder.

In another place, a simple cup of coffee was never before worshiped to the degree it was on the morning of the "Four Below Freeze-out."

This particular winter canoe/camp trip along the Au Sable River remains noteworthy for the extreme conditions confronting John and me when morning pack-up time arrived.

So cold was the air that we could only fumble with stuffing our sleeping bags for a few futile moments before our fingers would demand twice as much time near to the campfire.

Our water had frozen in its plastic jug. A giant creamberg had sprouted in our pint carton of half & half. And for much of our float we navigated among ice floes on the river.

But then came the warmth of the home, the warmth of the hospitality from Harleigh and Jan Pattullo, the warmth of the mug of coffee they offered each of us.

"Goodness" has never been more precisely defined.

Neither has "tradition," not as well as with that first Saturday morning at the Shamrock cup of coffee back in November of 1982.

Using the time-honored, sad-eyed, puppy dog routine, I had finagled an invitation to join Kal Jabara for my first duck hunt ever. Hunting Friday afternoon, we returned across the St. Clair River the next morning. On a day that would have been excellent for duck hunting, I drove through the rain and the wind into Utica, not ready yet to return home. Noticing Joe's car was already parked in its spot at the Sham, I tapped on the window, made sad puppy-dog eyes, and gained entrance.

Joe offered a cup of coffee, and owing either to our twenty-five year friendship or to the sadness with which I was gazing at the bottle of Bailey's Irish Cream, he set the bottle down in front of me, like a saloonkeeper in a western.

Soon it was Joe's turn to make sad eyes when he learned how much fortification my coffee needs. Now, he only leaves the Bailey's unattended in front of me at Christmas and on my birthday.

No matter. If any bill collector really needed to find me, all he'd have to do is to stake out the Shamrock Pub on any Saturday that I'm in town.

In fact, I drink more coffee at the Sham now than any alcoholic stuff. Even though I've cut way down on beer since the bicycle accident, however, I'd be remiss if I didn't mention a couple prime suds go-rounds shared with my father-in-law Charles.

Nothing has ever seemed so right and so welcome as the cold, wet blessing we gave ourselves in Ely, Minnesota, on the summer afternoon after we had paddled out of the Boundary Waters Canoe Area.

We had begun breaking camp at four that morning. Why not? Since midnight each of us had tried, unsuccessfully, to fool the other into believing that the monstrous storm was not keeping us awake. The nylon tent had strained and shuddered about as violently as—well, about as violently as you'd expect a three-man mountain tent to shudder in a wind whose other leg was kicking up tornadoes a hundred miles to the south.

Several times the tent had seemed ready to be launched into space. The only problem with that, of course, was that Charles and I would be part of the payload. Retreat seemed the best strategy.

Note: in a storm, heading from land to water hardly counts as "retreat." Paddling out, we stupidly crossed from one point to another without bothering to get into a lee. I couldn't tell, when we finally reached calm water, if my knees were trembling from all the weight I had put on them while hunkered down in the canoe paddling and praying, from the anxiety produced by that crossing, or from the anger that rose when Charles waited until we were a good mile from any shore to inform me that the last time he had been in a canoe was when, for fun as teenagers, he and his buddies tried tipping one over in the St. Clair River.

At any rate, simple pleasures immediately gained new importance. And upon our return to town, a celebratory quaff and a sip in thanksgiving seemed most appropriate.

And another celebration was what Charles and I treated ourselves to, the November afternoon we popped open a few cans in his dining room. His home's in Algonac, a short ferry ride across the river from the St. Clair Flats Wildlife Area.

We had experienced a rare day: with more than an hour of legal hunting time left, we had packed up and headed out, fully satisfied with the day's take, though each of us was a duck short of his legal limit.

A knock at the door interrupted our replay of a shot, and in walked "Bud" Jackson, Charles' neighbor, mother to my brother-in-law Jackson. Mrs. J. stopped by with some conversation and a German chocolate cake for Charles.

I don't believe he got a chance to sample how tasty that small cake was.

Especially when washed down with a chaser of cold beer.

About the Author

Humorist, storyteller, reporter, a dog's best friend—there is no single hook on which Tom Carney hangs his writer's hat. For over a decade he has been entertaining audiences with a writing style that blends observation, sensitivity, insight, and wit.

Currently, Carney writes a column for the *Oakland Press* in southeastern Michigan. As often as possible, he heads to his northern Michigan cabin where he, his wife Maureen, and their two English setters Maggie and Lucy most enjoy their sun-drenched days, two-blanket nights.